# Edwin T. Dahlberg:
# Pastor, Peacemaker, Prophet

## Second Edition

## Keith Dahlberg

*Foreword by Paul Raushenbush*

JUDSON PRESS
PUBLISHERS SINCE 1824
VALLEY FORGE, PA

Edwin T. Dahlberg: Pastor, Peacemaker, Prophet, Second Edition
© 2010 by Judson Press, Valley Forge, PA 19482-0851
© 1998 by Judson Press, Valley Forge, PA 19482-0851

ISBN: 978-0-8170-1277-9 (hardback)

**Library of Congress Cataloging-in-Publication Data**

Dahlberg, Keith.
　　Edwin T. Dahlberg : pastor, peacemaker, prophet / Keith Dahlberg ; foreword by Paul Raushenbush. -- 2nd ed.
　　　　p. cm.
　　Includes bibliographical references and index.
　　ISBN 978-0-8170-1660-9 (pbk. : alk. paper)  1. Dahlberg, Edwin T. (Edwin Theodore), 1892–1986. 2. Baptists--United States--Clergy--Biography. I. Title.

BX6495.D25D34　2010
286'.1092—dc22
[B]
　　　　　　　　　　　　　　　　　　　　　　　　　　　　　　　2010017054

Printed in the U.S.A.
First Edition, 2010.

Become a Friend of Judson.
Visit www.friendsofjudson.org

*To seminary students and their spouses:*
*the next generation*

# Contents

Edwin T. Dahlberg

# Foreword

History is made by the actions of extraordinary individuals who influence the world in their own time to such a degree that those of us living after them still benefit from their inspiration and commitment. The late Rev. Edwin T. Dahlberg was clearly such an extraordinary individual, and we are fortunate to have this excellent biography by his son, Keith. Reading this book is like being offered a front-row seat on a historical journey. It is a journey that traverses the classic American immigrant search for religious freedom, from the hard work of a family in a new land, to a call to ministry, and into the most important religious debates and political movements of the mid-twentieth century.

Edwin Dahlberg was senior pastor of some of America's preeminent Baptist churches. He played a leadership role in the Northern Baptist Convention, the Fellowship of Reconciliation, the Baptist Peace Fellowship, and the World Council of Churches, and he served as president of the National Council of Churches of Christ (1957–60).

Like a first rate journalist, Keith Dahlberg has recorded his father's involvement in these often contentious and controversial organizations, and this memoir features frequent "aha" moments when a piece of a puzzle that had been missing is snapped into place. As an American Baptist myself, I have never before read such a concise and compelling description of the Liberal-Conservative debates that swirled within my own denomination in the mid 1940s, and which continue to play out in the twenty-first century.

Rev. Dahlberg was a radical. At an early age he made the decision to become a conscientious objector—in World War I! It was an unflinching commitment to peace that he maintained all of his life. He recognized the sin of racism from the beginning of his ministry, and while other preachers were writing to Dr. Martin Luther King Jr. with the patronizing advice to go slow, Rev. Dahlberg was one of the few who wrote a much-needed letter of support while Dr. King was in the notorious Birmingham jail. It was an act of solidarity for which King was always thankful.

Rev. Dahlberg insisted that it was not a contradiction for a Christian to have deep religious convictions and a thriving spiritual life while also holding liberal views about scriptural inerrancy and an inclusive approach to other religious traditions. His religious convictions sometimes brought hardship and attack, but Dahlberg had the gospel on his side, which carried him through the storms.

In the most public way possible, Rev. Dahlberg lived out his faith, and by leading with such lauded integrity, he inspired others to follow. Vignettes in this book, such as those describing when Rev. Dahlberg brought a deeply divided church back together or tamed a virulent opponent to the NCC by having lunch with him, offer the reader a practical "how to" manual for maintaining one's own convictions while still valuing reconciliation and allowing the other side to feel heard and respected. It is no surprise that Rev. Dahlberg was continually asked to stay on for a second term as leader of important organizations, and whenever he moved on to a new pastorate, his leaving was always mourned by his previous congregation.

Yet what makes this book so captivating is not the public life of Pastor Dahlberg, but the day-to-day manner in which he went about his life as a Christian. We learn about the true nature of Dahlberg when we read of his gentle encouragement of a young Keith to find not merely a pretty wife but someone who was also a true soul mate. We perceive the deep love Edwin shared with his first wife until her death, and then the joy he felt when finding a second woman with whom he could live out the rest of his days. We recognize his matter-of-fact pastoral impulse when he got out of a car to steady a drunken man.

While it is certainly true that Rev. Dahlberg is a historical figure whose memory we should honor, we should also make sure that we each listen closely to Dahlberg's response to the desperate cry of a boy in a psychiatric ward who repeatedly cried out, "Am I done for?" To the sick boy, Pastor Dahlberg spoke with assurance: "No, you are not done for. God loves you." In those simple, pastoral, Christian words, we find the true meaning of the life of Rev. Edwin T. Dahlberg.

Rev. Dahlberg studied under my great-grandfather while in seminary, and this biography gets Walter Rauschenbusch just right. Keith Dahlberg is careful to show that Rauschenbusch cared deeply for the well being of each person as well as for the society in which the individual resides—it was never a choice between one concern or the other. Dahlberg was ordained the year of Rauschenbusch's death, and he continued to carry the torch that Rauschenbusch passed, a fire that still burns, although alas, the light is fainter than it was. Reading this memoir one can't help but wince at our own tepidness in contrast with the passion and radical commitment of Rauschenbusch and Dahlberg. How many Christians, and specifically Baptists, have decided that it is better to be safe than courageous, to be pious rather than righteous?

My prayer is that this book might reignite that passion for establishing justice and creating a world that reflects God's abiding love for each individual. May *Edwin T. Dahlberg—Pastor, Peacemaker, and Prophet* continue to impart inspiration and faith to our generation and generations to come.

Paul Brandeis Raushenbush
Princeton University, 2010

# Preface to the Second Edition

When I first started writing my father's biography in 1996, a family member gently told me I was too late. After all, he had died ten years previously at age 93, and few of his contemporaries were still alive to remember him. But I was convinced that my father's life is one of those rare lives worth remembering, even decades after he left this earth, not only by friends and family, but by younger men and women whose lives have been touched by his life and thought. And now, nearly twenty-five years after his passing, I remain confident that still later generations will be influenced by the legacy of his beliefs, his teachings, and his life.

Certain human and spiritual values unite men and women of good will in all races, languages, and religions, even beyond pragmatic needs for food, good health, education, and so on. There are also spiritual needs: nourishment for the soul, help when humanity fails us, the need to seek and find God. These spiritual necessities are often obscured, even denied, by those around us who are distracted by the speed and demands of twenty-first century life. Amid all this, we sometimes need a reminder of God's call, "Here is the path, walk in it."

Edwin T. Dahlberg's life of calm and caring competence is that kind of reminder, worth examining.

Keith Dahlberg
March 2010

# Preface

This book started a memoir for my family, by which a younger generation could learn about their grandfather. Edwin T. Dahlberg wrote family letters about events in his life and in the world around him. Gathered into sequence, they disclose a history of which I had been only dimly aware when growing up (I am one of his sons). Curiosity led me to research other collections of his papers as well as the recollections of his colleagues.

My father talked with presidents, made a spirited public defense of the church against charges of communist infiltration, gave leadership to the search for peace in a nation more and more preoccupied with war. He involved himself in all this at the same time that he served competently as the pastor of a large church. Indeed, he applied uncommon expertise to his everyday job of minister of the gospel, not only in preaching, but also in counseling, administration, and public relations.

He had two other characteristics, often ignored when professionals are appraised: he was dependably available and accessible. The two terms are not synonymous. *Available* means keeping predictable office hours, answering phone calls, replying to mail. *Accessible* means exhibiting receptive friendliness, having an open ear, being willing to address the problem at hand. In short, individuals could find him, and they felt welcome. These talents are not easy to maintain in the face of fatigue, conflicting demands, and hostile criticism. Someone who keeps his or her act together this well is, by definition, a worthwhile role model.

This book attempts to illumine what made my father tick. It tries to identify the chief decision points in his life. The story often digresses, watching him catch gophers, talk with drunks, greet people at the door, issue an altar call, debate prayer in the schools. It examines his mastery of the art of reconciliation, which was respected by national leaders in Congress, industry, trade unions, and the Pentagon.

Not everyone approved of or respected him and his work. Some confronted him with placards: "Atheist! Communist! Integrationist!" A frustrated FBI agent once said of him, "I've been trying to get something on that SOB for twenty years!"[1]

Pressure rarely bothered Dad. He enjoyed living in the world, enjoyed his work. He considered it logical to live what the Bible teaches. He believed anyone could live this way, with the help of God, and he devoted much effort to help people see this about themselves. He knew where his own roots were anchored, among the Swedish farmers and tradespeople who came to America seeking religious freedom, and he was able to hold a vision of what the world could be. How compatible his vision is with present "reality" is for each reader to decide.

There remains one point to deal with here: how to refer to my father. "Dad" seems most natural to me, but it is an illogical designation for a child or young bachelor in the early chapters. I have, therefore, chosen to make the transition from "Edwin" or "Dahlberg" (young men of that era frequently addressed one another by last name) to "Dad" at about the point in the narrative when I was born.

# Acknowledgments

For many years, Edwin T. Dahlberg wrote weekly letters to his children whenever he or they were away from home. In addition, files of speeches, diaries, news clippings, work correspondence, and other memorabilia fill fifteen linear feet of shelf space at the American Baptist Historical Society in Rochester, New York, even before all the family papers are gathered in. The problem was, not gathering data, but sifting it for the turning points in his life and the people and events that influenced him.

I am grateful to his wife Viola (my stepmother) and my cousin Dorothy Cordwell for sitting down with Dad when he was in his eighties and tape recording recollections of his early life. As far as records are available, the facts and the gist of conversations in the early chapters are correct and based on my father's and grandfather's notes. The first account (in the north Swedish province of Norrbotten) happened to another family, not ours, but their story reveals the tension of that era in Sweden and the reasons why many Swedes emigrated.

I am grateful to my niece Gail Randall for the loan of letters from her grandfather and am thankful for the letters loaned by Maline Balian Broberg of St. Paul and for the letters and church bulletins saved by the late Helen Compton of St. Louis. Photographs came from my cousins Dorothy Cordwell, Grace Gibson, and Marion Dergance and from my nieces Judy Brasch and Gail Randall, as well as from the archives of the National Council of Churches (NCC) and the Ameircan Baptist Historical Society, and from Polly DeLima, archivist at First Baptist Church, Syracuse. So many family members have contributed photographs, letters, and reminiscences that this book has really become a sort of clan effort. Dad's colleagues also responded generously to requests for their memories, among them Paul C. Allen, Lois Brackman, Woodrow Clark, Beverly Davison, Richard Deats, Roger Fredrikson. Billy James Hargis, Paul Lewis, LaRue Loughhead, Doward McBain, Martha Miller, Dennis Norris, Robert Remington, and John Schroeder.

Deep-felt thanks go to my brother, Bruce, for his helpful contributions and comments and to my sister, Margaret Torgersen, and her husband, Gordon, who contributed valuable insights into Dad's professional and personal character, even though their modesty limits mention of some of their own work.

I owe a great deal to Dana Martin and Jim Lynch and the staff at the American Baptist Historical Society and to Sarah Vilankulu at NCC headquarters.

Many thanks to Sallye Prenger, who took time out of her several simultaneous careers to critique the manuscript for both style and substance, and to the editorial staff at Judson Press, particularly Mary Nicol, Kristy Pullen, Victoria McGoey, Ruthann Dwyer, and Tina Edginton, all of whom showed much patience in helping refine the final manuscript.

Finally, I appreciate the time and work contributed by my wife, Lois, by my children, Susan, Patricia, John, and Nancy, and by others who have gone over the manuscript and have spoken out frankly when changes were needed.

# Chapter 1

# Sweden

*In the latter half of the nineteenth century in Sweden, economic hard times and religious conflict combined to cause a million Swedes—one-seventh of the population—to seek their fortunes in other lands. The initial stimulus was often a combination of state and church laws.*

## Norrbotten Province, about 1852

At the knock on the door, the farmer slowly got up from where he had been sitting with his wife by the cradle, watching their young son sleep. He opened the cabin door to see the village pastor, accompanied by the town police officer, who was looking uncomfortable. "Good afternoon, Erik!" The pastor's tone was a little overhearty. "It's been a long time since I've had a chance to visit with you. We miss you in church. May I, . . . er, may we come in?"

"Yah, sure, Reverend, please come in, both of you. Sit down. Constable, you've met my wife, Inge? And this is little Anders." The policeman nodded at the woman. He looked as if he wished he were somewhere else.

"You know, Reverend," the farmer continued as they all sat, "we don't really consider ourselves Lutheran any more. We have joined the new Baptist congregation. It's not like we aren't going to church."

"Erik, in Sweden, the Lutherans are the church. You are still Swedish, aren't you?"

"Yah . . ."

"Well!" the minister's voice grew even heartier, "There you are, then! Erik, Inge, it's time your child was baptized—past time."

"No, Reverend, we Baptists believe each person shall choose, when he is of an age to make the choice for himself. We are going to try to teach Anders to love God and have a strong faith as he grows up, but he will choose for himself whether to be baptized."

"But he must be baptized. It is the law! Inge, surely you can see?"

"You can't make someone a Christian by decree!" Inge was quietly defiant. Protective.

"It is the will of God and the King!"

"The King's maybe. Not God's. We believe in the freedom of each person to choose."

"Yes, well, it is the law, and that is what we are here to do. Come, Constable!" The pastor rose and picked the baby up out of his cradle, as the constable stood between him and the distraught parents. "You both may come, too, of course." And he took the baby to church to be baptized.[1]

Two weeks later the pastor was back. "You have not paid the bill for the child's baptism."

"We do not intend to pay it. All this is contrary to our religious faith. The only way you can get any payment is the same way you took the baby out of his cradle—by force!"

"As you wish." The pastor and the constable went out to the barn and presently reappeared, leading the family's only cow on a rope.

Erik stood in the door of the cabin, grim, his arm around his weeping wife's shoulders, as they watched their cow disappear. "The mayor accused me of treason, yesterday. He said the state church gets a good bit of revenue from registering baptisms, marriages, and burials and said heretics like us are going to ruin the country. Wanted to know if I had heard about the mob stoning some Baptists down south last month. He sounded like he'd be happy to give me all the details."

"Erik, what are we going to do?"

"I've been thinking a lot about this lately. Praying about it, too. They say that there is good land, and freedom, too, across the ocean. They say parts of America are a lot like Sweden. Maybe we should go. We should stand by our beliefs."

## Bohult, Småland Province, 1869: The Danielson Family

Nils Danielson glumly surveyed his accounts of the year's crops. Smålenings are supposed to be able to make a living on a rock in the middle of the sea, according to the old proverb. Such thrift was certainly needed, Nils reflected—the fruit crop had done all right, with even some left over to take to market. As for the rest of his acreage of stumps, bogs, and stones, only the livestock were doing passably well, and that thanks to young Elof, with his shepherd's fife and his sundial. Carl-Johan—Charlie—his oldest boy, had gone off to America to seek his fortune last spring, and August and Anna-Maria would soon find that they had their own lives to live.[2] "It gets a little harder each year," he thought. And it did not help any at all for the neighbors to turn hostile.

The ill will had started when Nils and his family joined the small group of Baptists that began in the nearby village of Bohult. It was not that he was angry with the Lutherans, but the state church had had nothing in its perfunctory church worship to help keep his own father off alcohol. The last straw had been when Father had come home drunk, Christmas Eve, and stumbled into the candlelighted Christmas tree, turning the holiday into a holocaust that had burned down the house.[3] The Baptist faith appeared to mean something to its believers, and life held more happiness now, despite the disapproval of his Lutheran neighbors.

Things had come to a head last Sunday evening. As was their custom, Nils and Johanna had invited the little congregation of Baptists to hold evening worship in their home. They had scarcely assembled when the opening words of the visiting lay preacher were interrupted by the rattle of stones striking the wall. Johanna peered out through the drawn curtain. "Some people from town, Pastor. They look angry . . ."

"It's not the first time people have objected to our worshiping God outside the Lutheran Church, Sister. Let us continue."

Someone pounded on the front door. "Police! Open up!"

Johanna quickly blew out all the candles. Another woman took her own shawl and threw it over the pastor's head and led him to the door. As she opened it, she said loudly enough for the crowd to hear, "Come, now, Grandma, it's time we were getting home!" The pair passed through the hostile neighbors without incident.[4]

"No one was hurt this time," Nils said to his family later. "But how long are we prepared to go on like this?"

"What choice do we have, Husband? This is home."

"What's it like where Charlie is, Father?" asked eleven-year-old Elof. "His letter sounds as if America is just like Sweden. Could we go there?"

Småland farmers consider carefully before they speak. "Start life over again at fifty years of age?" Nils became lost in thought. Anna and her brother August looked interested. A new life, away from the growing hostility and poverty of Småland, "the impoverished land." There was silence in the room. Johanna finally ventured, "What are you thinking, Nils?"

Nils stroked his jaw, slowly. "Yaw-w . . . ," he murmured. More silence. The family watched his face, intent on his decision. Then, finally, "Yaw-w . . . we just might!"

## Varburg, Skåne Province, 1868: The Ring Family

Hans Ringius was a small man, ex-army, who preferred to be called Ring, army style. In a country full of Christophersons, Ingemannsons, Johansons, and the like, the Swedish military had long ago discovered that roll call went faster if each recruit was assigned a one-syllable name. Hans Ring liked it that way.[5] He had built up a good trade in tailoring since getting out of the army, and even had a sideline as a vaccinator. A tailor always had a needle handy, and he needed only to carry a small vial containing a pox scab. He would pierce the scab with the needle, scratch a child's arm, and the job was done.[6]

The land around Malmo was fertile and the times prosperous. If it were not for neighbors fighting each other about religion, he reflected, the times were not bad at all. Not that he regretted having become a Baptist some ten years before. He had no quarrel with the Lutherans himself; after all, he had met his Elna when she worked for Pastor Wisselgren. But things had come to a fine mess when his daughter had chosen to be baptized last year and had to be immersed under a bridge at midnight, to avoid being stoned by some of the townspeople.[7]

Anna had been eighteen years old and knew her own mind. He had always felt capable of handling himself—but to have his children damned as heretics, and even traitors! There must be a better way for them to grow up.

Minnesota, now. Over in America, the New World. They say the religions can get along over there—Lutherans and Baptists and all kinds, side by side. The government did not try to stick its oar in. Elna's mother and the other daughters had gone in 1857 and said the rolling farmland was just like Sweden. She had mentioned some Indian wars a few years back; had had a close call with some Indians herself one afternoon, washing clothes down by the lake, but he guessed things had quieted down now.

Minnesota. Fertile farmland. Freedom to worship as they believed God wanted them to. Not much demand there for Swedish army dress uniforms, his specialty in trade. Have to work harder to make a living, probably, but he could be a farmer if he had to. And Anna, Mary, and Christina would have a good, safe place to grow up . . .

Men of Skåne needed little time to come to a decision once the choices lay before them. It would be good to live in a place like that! *Yu, yu men!* "Yes indeed!"

# Chapter 2

# Minnesota

*The Danielson and Ring families, still strangers to each other, chose Minnesota because of its resemblance to farm country back home. Their hardships in establishing themselves in the new country typify the frontier and helped form the character of their descendants.[1]*

## St. Paul, 1870: The Danielsons

It hadn't been all that bad a journey so far. The 144 acres at Bohult had gone for a good price to a newly married young couple, and the cattle, sheep, bees, threshing machine, and everything else that they could not carry had been sold at public auction.

Anna-Maria had been busy weaving for weeks, producing new dress goods, linen, tablecloths, and shawls to add to the family supply. Johanna and Nils had packed all the household supplies in ironbound crates for the long trip; Carl-Johan had written that everything in America was very costly after the recent Civil War. "An impressive stack of boxes and baggage," thought Nils. "It's going to be a big job getting it to Carl-Johan's when we get to the end of the railroad." It *had* been a job at each transfer point so far, from a borrowed wagon in Bohult to the railroad, again at Malmo and across the Skattegat to Copenhagen; another ferry to Germany, one transshipment after another till they had finally boarded the Inman Line steamer *SS City of Brooklyn* at Liverpool along with 1,500 other passengers bound for New York.

There had been enough other immigrants on the train for Chicago that Nils's lack of knowledge of the English language had not been a problem. Indeed, the only risk so far had been in Chicago, where a Swedish hotel man had got on the train and in Swedish issued an expansive invitation to one and all to come to his hotel. "I always entertain my own countrymen when they pass through Chicago," he announced. "I have rigs here at the depot, plenty for all of you and your baggage, and I am glad to convey everyone to my hotel!" At the hotel he had invited all the men to enjoy themselves in the bar with drinks and card playing. "You can have a bang-up time in this new country," he said. But Smålenings had not survived by being gullible. Nils had been suspicious of this freely offered friendship and, with true backwoods Swedish caution, decided it would be better for his purse if he moved his family to another hotel, where they stayed over Sunday.

Now that they had arrived in St. Paul, however, Nils had a more serious problem. Carl-Johan was nowhere to be found. Nils was sure he had written his son the correct date of their arrival. The children did not mind the wait; there was always plenty to see in this new country for Anna, August, and young Elof. But as the day wore on, Nils decided that there was no point in standing around the station. They would get a hotel for the night, and maybe Carl-Johan would show up in the morning.

As was discovered later, the storekeeper-postmaster in the little village of Evansville, Minnesota, had taken the letter addressed to Carl-Johan Nilson and put it in a pigeonhole in his desk at the post office and then forgotten about it. Nearly everyone in that country was a Nelson or an Anderson or a Johnson, and the postmaster had a big area to the west to which he had to forward mail, often with little detail on the envelope as to where the addressee might be found. The letter was never delivered.

Nils waited for his son for a whole week in St. Paul before deciding that they had better go on. People at the hotel had advised him that the train could take him as far as the current railhead at Wilmar, one hundred miles west, and he could no doubt hire a wagon there to take him on to his destination at Dayton Hollow, wherever that might be out on the plains. Once more, they boarded a train and headed west.

"Can I help you?" The stationmaster at Wilmar spoke Swedish to Nils, after he saw that nothing much would be accomplished in English.

"Yaw, if you would, please. My name is Nils Danielson. I am looking for my son, Carl-Johan Nilson, twenty-three years old. We should have met him back at St. Paul, but he never showed up. I thought he might have left word here."

"No . . . not that I know of. He live here in Wilmar?"

"He has a farm in Dayton Hollow. What do you call it, he has home-steaded there."

"Dayton Hollow. George! You ever hear of a place called Dayton Hollow?"

"Way up north, somewhere," came a voice from the baggage room. "Otter Tail country, I think. 'Bout a hundred miles."

"Looks like you still have some traveling to do, Mister."

"Is there a livery stable where we might hire a wagon for the journey, then?"

"Yes, there's a place you can hire a wagon, but you can't take a wagon over the plains at this time of year. It's been a wet spring. About the only way you're going to get there is walk. You can store your freight here in the station till things dry out enough to pull a wagon. How much of a pile is it?"

"About two thousand pounds, the ship line told me. I would be very grateful if you would store everything here. I'll be back for it as soon as I can."

He returned to his family. "Well, Johanna, children, we have a long walk ahead of us."

"How will we know the way, Father?"

"We'll have to ask people we meet."

Carrying just enough bedding and clothing to protect them from the cool May nights, the Danielsons started walking toward a homestead shanty they could see on the north horizon. To their dismay, they encoun-tered a river, brimming full with the spring runoff, between them and the shanty. As they paused to consider this unexpected obstacle, a man came running toward them from the west where the rail line was under con-struction. "You trying to steal my boat?" he shouted at the bewildered travelers. Nils soon convinced the man that they had not even seen his boat, but just wanted to get across the river. The man had a small skiff hidden in the reeds and for a dollar rowed the family across in two trips. They were able to continue their trek.

August came up to his little brother, whose job it was to carry the water bottle. "How about a drink, Elof?"

Elof grinned. "Drink all you want. The more you drink, the less I have to carry! August, did you see all the fish in that river we crossed? This is going to be good country!"

Without a map, the route to Dayton Hollow was uncertain. It was a remarkable accomplishment for Nils to trek a hundred miles on foot cross-country with his wife and children, carrying their food and bedrolls, and to make the journey in a week. The first half of the journey was through prairie grass, swampy areas, and small lakes. Low hills stretched to the horizon, and there was rarely a settler anywhere along the way to show the Danielsons the route. Sometimes they found themselves miles off course to the east or the west. They hoped that Dayton Hollow really was to the north, as the station man had thought, and that they would be able to find Charlie when they reached it. It wasn't like Charlie not to leave word anywhere, but they were from Småland and had faith in God. It probably did not occur to them to give up. Each night around the camp-fire, Nils would read a chapter from the Bible with the family and pray before they slept.

Making about twenty miles a day, the Danielsons eventually reached a beautiful lake and the town of Glenwood. After that it was easier going. Arriving at Chippewa Station, they met a Mr. Kronberg from Evansville. They gladly accepted his invitation to come home with him and stay over Sunday.

Charlie, meanwhile, had been waiting for the letter from his parents that never arrived. He finally set out for St. Paul in hopes of hearing some word about his family. At Glenwood, someone told him a family of that description had passed through that morning, heading for Chippewa Station. Heading back northwest, he got word from the storekeeper at Chippewa and arrived at the Kronberg house long after dark. He pound-ed on the door, and the family was finally reunited.

All day Sunday, the family talked and planned. Carl-Johan told his family how he had arrived in Minnesota in 1869 with his friend Christian Johnson from back home and how they had walked cross-country from Duluth to settle in western Minnesota. Though he had homesteaded 160 acres for only a year, he was already prospering. On Monday, father and son went out and bought a yoke of oxen, a wagon, a sod-breaking plow, tools, and provisions. Mr. Kronberg, who had taken a liking to the boys, presented them with a pup named Jeff. They started out the next morning with the wagon full of their purchases for the last thirty miles of their journey, arriving in Dayton Hollow on 18 May 1870.

The next week, after putting almost his last dollars into land purchase, Nils started back for Wilmar with the oxen and wagon to fetch his stored freight, taking his youngest son with him. As Nils expected, the trip back went faster than the walk, but the town looked different somehow when he arrived. He felt disoriented at first, thinking he was perhaps on the wrong street, and then he saw the blackened stumps of timbers and the gray ashes where the railroad station had been. Numbly, he pulled the oxen to the side of the road, got out, and stood looking at the remains of the building that had held the results of all the family's months of labor. Bedding, clothing, all of Anna's weaving, pots and pans, tools, mementos of the past, all were gone. He scraped a mound of ashes slowly with the toe of his boot; surely he could not have lost everything? He bent down to pick up a piece of gray metal. A key to one of his chests. The only thing left . . .

A voice sounded behind Nils, "You lose some freight in the fire, friend?"

"Yaw . . . everything my family had . . . I don't know what to do now."

"Well," responded the man gruffly but gently, "you'd probably best go to that building down the street there. The station agent has set up a temporary office. A lot of folks lost things here last week."

Nils was a large man, but his shoulders slumped as he trudged over to the temporary office. The stationmaster looked up from the table that was serving him as a makeshift desk. He looked tired and a little grim. "Yes, sir?"

Nils was still dazed. "All my family's belongings. They were all in the station. I don't know what to do."

The stationmaster sighed, rubbed a hand over his eyes. "You'd better fill out this paper. List everything you can remember. The railroad will pay damages, but it won't be the full value of when the things were new."

With the help of the stationmaster, Nils made an itemized list. His two thousand pounds of freight, even in those days, was worth more than a thousand dollars. In the end, he had to settle for two hundred.

He walked back to the wagon where Elof was tending the oxen. "I guess our business is finished here, son. We'd best be starting home."

"What will we do for all the things we lost, Father?"

"We'll trust in God, Elof. We've done that before and never had any cause to be disappointed." He wheeled the oxen around, and they started the hundred miles home.

To compound the family's troubles that first summer, Nils returned to find Johanna suffering from a serious illness, from which she took two months to recover and which left her hearing permanently damaged.

That first winter was hard. But the Danielsons were fortunate in having good neighbors who helped them with bedding and clothing to fend off the cold. It was true, what they had speculated back in Sweden: far from the theological fights of the old country, Lutherans and Baptists and others worked together. Nils and Johanna were encouraged to find several Baptist neighbors, and with eight others that first year, they founded a small church. It was the first church in the new community of Fergus Falls when that town formed the following year two miles north of them. Nils sent young Elof off to school, having first ascertained that schools of this new country had no government-sponsored prayer as there had been back in Sweden.

Considering all of their initial setbacks, the Danielson family fared very well the following year. Though they had lost most of their possessions, they had enough compensation money left to buy provisions and a couple of cows. Nils homesteaded his own 160 acres next to his son's, borrowing, when his own funds were depleted, from one of the town businessmen at 24-percent interest. Rather than pale at such a risk, Nils took it in stride, for farmers from Småland were a thrifty lot who knew their capabilities.

The family did make one basic change regarding their surnames. Swedish custom in the old country was for the children to take the first name of the father and add "son" or "dotter," as the case may be. Many of Nils's neighbors retained the old names and kept getting their mail mixed up. It had finally reached the point at which some of them had to be distinguished by their trade, so that there was a Picture-frame Carlson and a Smoked-Fish Johnson in town. Nils's own grandfather had been Eskil Anderson, and his father was named Daniel Eskilson. He, therefore, was Nils Danielson, and his children were Carl-Johan, August, and Elof Nilsson and Anna-Maria Nilsdotter. But Nils was tired of all the confusion with other Nelsons, Danielsons, and all, who probably made up at least half the population, and he adopted the American custom of all the generations having the same surname. Recalling the hills of Småland, Nils chose the name Dahlberg, which in Swedish meant something like "valley in the mountains." And the name was sufficiently uncommon to give his family some identity.

The pioneer Dahlbergs prospered through hard work, health, and belief that God would take care of them if they, in turn, trusted God. They built a shack, that first year, in which they lived for two years. The boys fished, trapped muskrat and mink, built a flatboat for the lake on the farm, and trapped ducks, earning enough to buy much of the family's provisions.

Besides doing their heavy farm work, the men earned money building the first bridge over the Ottertail River and built a house for one of their neighbors. Teenage Elof could earn up to $1.75 a day packing shingles at Wright's sawmill. The fields yielded two wagon loads of wheat in 1871, and the men traded some of their bread and butter with the Indians for furs. In 1872, Nils hauled logs out of the woods, smoothed them on both sides, and built what the family agreed was the best house around, with floors, shingles, windows, and doors hauled in from Alexandria, fifty miles away. Nils then borrowed from the bank at 18-percent interest enough to buy an additional 240 acres of prime farmland at $5 an acre. The men spent the winter cutting poles and had the entire farm fenced the following spring. That year, they broke sixty acres of sod, using a sixteen-inch plow hitched to three yoke of oxen.

The years did not bring an unbroken string of rewards. While the Dahlberg men were busy with the sod breaking, a warm wind brought millions of grasshoppers in from the Dakota country, covering the earth and the fence posts, eating everything in sight. Elof claimed that when they left their work jackets in the field to go home for lunch, only the brass buttons remained when they returned. For some reason, the grasshoppers would not touch the pea vines, but everything else was destroyed that summer. The insects laid their eggs that fall, and the next spring the newly hatched hoppers destroyed one hundred acres of wheat. The situation was widespread and so serious that Minnesota's Governor Pillsbury called for a statewide three-day period of prayer. About that time, another west wind arose, carrying the grasshopper horde eastward into Lake Superior and Lake Michigan.

And then there was the blizzard of 1873. Minnesotans define a blizzard as a heavy wind-blown snowstorm with the temperature lower than zero degrees Fahrenheit. This one met all the criteria, and it lasted three days. A clothesline had to be strung between house and stable in order for someone to get out and feed the stock, but the animals had to stay inside without water for two days. One of the men got lost in the blizzard but survived by stumbling into a sheepfold and bedding down among the sheep.

## Fergus Falls, 1879

As the years went by, Nils Dahlberg was well satisfied with the choice he and his family had made back in Småland. Anna had found a husband almost immediately. It might even be said that Sven Hellander had pursued her to Fergus Falls since he had come over from the old country on the same boat and just happened to homestead a couple of miles away. August had soon found his mate in Louise Larson, and after they married, Nils split the four-hundred-acre farm, with Elof and himself working one of the halves and August the other. Charlie had married Carolina Svenson the year after his family had joined him, but Charlie always seemed to have an eye for far horizons. He sold his farm in 1879, packed up his wife and four children, and took off for San Francisco, and later Astoria, Oregon.

That left Elof, now twenty, who didn't seem to see anyone special among the girls around Fergus Falls. "If only the boy wasn't so shy," thought Nils. "He's a hard enough worker and good-looking enough. Sometimes I'd like to push him out the door and tell him, 'Don't come back till you find her!'"

Nils and Johanna realized that the religious problems that had plagued them in Sweden had followed them in a sense. Not that their Lutheran neighbors gave them any trouble, but they had hoped their children would continue in the faith in which they had grown up. They talked it over one night with the traveling Baptist preacher whom they occasionally invited to stay overnight when he came through. "Pastor, you've traveled around Minnesota a lot. Don't you know any nice Swedish Baptist girl who'd make a good wife for our Elof?"

The preacher stared into the fire and thought for a few minutes. "Yes," he said slowly, "the Rings down in Grove City have three fine girls. Annie is already married, I believe. But Mary, the second daughter, she would make your Elof a good wife. Those girls are good cooks, too!"

Nils and Johanna wrote a letter to these strangers a hundred miles away, told them of their hope that their son might find a good Baptist girl, such apparently being in short supply around their part of Minnesota, and asked if the Rings would be willing for Elof to pay Mary a visit, with a possible view to marriage. In due course, a gracious letter arrived in Fergus Falls, saying the Rings would be very pleased to have Elof come.

Elof seemed agreeable to this adventure. One winter morning, wearing a new raccoon-skin fur coat against the cold weather, he boarded the train for Grove City.

## Grove City, 1879

Hans Ring had had his doubts when his family first joined Elna's mother and sisters, who had come several years earlier than his own arrival in 1868. Old Elsa, his mother-in-law, had quite a few wild experiences during the Sioux wars, and his own children had listened with wide eyes and open ears to her stories.

The Indians had made a treaty with the United States government, ceding all their land in Minnesota and northern Iowa at twelve cents per acre, except for a ten-mile-wide strip reserved for them along the Minnesota River. Given the size of the land, this still amounted to quite a bit of money, but the Indians were not accustomed to the ways of traders who sold them goods at high prices and then sought, and got, first lien on the government payments, leaving little for the Indians to live on. The fighting that broke out in 1862 probably had its roots in a number of factors: starving Indians, unscrupulous traders, incompetent government agents, poorly garrisoned forts, and a national government preoccupied with the Civil War. Only about two hundred soldiers held the 370 miles of frontier from the Canadian line to Iowa.

> It began right here in Meeker County [Old Elsa told her enthralled grandchildren]. A band of hungry Indians were hunting near the Jones place, over to Acton. They had been arguing among themselves and finally came up to Rob Jones and asked for whiskey. Now whiskey is something no settler in his right mind would give to an Indian, 'specially one who was already in a temper, and Mr. Jones of course said no. So the Indians challenged Rob and Howard Baker, his neighbor, to a target-shooting contest. The Indians told our men to shoot first, which they did. Before they could reload, the Indians shot and killed them. Killed Mrs. Jones, too, but Mrs. Baker and her baby fell back wounded into the cellar and pretended to be dead. Your Uncle Ola had come to the Acton store that morning for supplies, and he was the first man on the scene after the shooting. Just happened by. He helped Mrs. Baker and the baby and then rode his horse to warn all the settlers into the fort at Forest City. Wasn't much of a fort, but it held off an Indian attack that night, and the only loss was about sixty-five horses and some burned-down buildings.

Little six-year-old Christina always had the most to say. "Do the Indians shoot at you, Grandmother?" "No, child," answered Old Elsa,

> we're mostly on good terms with the Indians except during that time. We trade them bread for muskrat skins, and sometimes if they have nothing to trade, we feed 'em anyway, just like you would anyone else. I had a good scare once, though.
>
> I was down by the lake, doing the laundry on the rocks by the shore when I looked up, and here come half a dozen Indians in war paint, with their bodies all covered with bacon grease and ashes to keep off the mosquitoes. I tell you, I was petrified! But I kept calm, wrung out the dress I had been scrubbing, and walked back to the house. The Indians followed right behind me! I'd

heard that they don't usually attack anybody at worship, so I went into the bedroom, got the family Bible, and came out and sat on a stump and read it, and then closed my eyes, folded my hands, and prayed. When I opened my eyes again, they were walking away down the shore single file, pointing up at the sky.

Hans, who had been leaning against the door frame as he listened to Old Elsa, knew that his mother-in-law was a lot luckier, or a lot more God protected, depending on how a person looked at it, than she seemed to realize. He was just as glad that things had calmed down before his own family had arrived. Made his own troubles with that shyster on the train seem pretty small . . .

The Rings had gotten off the boat at Quebec City and boarded the train for the West. It had scarcely left the station before this big man asked to see everybody's tickets. Looking over the tickets of the Ring family, the man handed them back to Hans and told him that they weren't for the complete trip, that he would have to pay more. Hans had smelled a rotten fish and told the man the tickets looked all right to him. The man became quite violent and was trying to get his hand in Hans's pocket when the whole family joined the battle. Hans grinned to himself in recollection of the scene. He was a small man, but with his army training he could give a good account of himself. But it was his Elna beating the man over the head with her umbrella, Anna and Mary kicking his shins, and even little Christina pulling at his coattails that had finally made the man retreat, cursing and vowing that they would be put off at the next station. As Hans had suspected, the man had nothing to do with the railroad. The real conductor came through a while later and said there was nothing wrong with the tickets.

For the Ring family, things had gone pretty well in the eleven years since leaving the old country. Farming was a lot harder work than tailoring, but they had done well. Anna had found a good husband in Peter Peterson. Now it looked as if nineteen-year-old Mary might have good prospects—if this Dahlberg boy turned out to be all right. Hans figured that Elof Dahlberg would be getting to Grove City the next day, for no one in his right mind would be coming right after last night's blizzard.

"Father, someone's coming across the field! Do you suppose it could be Elof?"

Hans warmed a spot on the window with his hand to peer out. "Not unless he's lost his way. Come to think of it, with this blizzard sweeping everything level, he might have done just that!"

"He looks like a big bear in that fur coat!" giggled seventeen-year-old Christina. She had been waiting to see this new swain of her sister's for some days and intended to give both of them as difficult a time as she could.

Suddenly, whoever it was out there disappeared completely under the snow, only to appear a few moments later looking like a polar bear. "He fell in the ditch!" laughed Christina delightedly. "It was all covered over, and he didn't see it!" This was going to be even more entertaining than she had expected.

"Hans, go out and help the boy!" This from Elna, who was mortified to have things start out this way. "He'll get pneumonia!"

In good humor, Hans went to the door, which the young man had reached by now, helped him brush off his coat, and sat him by the fire to warm up. "I really should have driven the horse and sleigh down to the station," thought Hans, "but who would have thought the boy had the grit to take the train in weather like this, much less walk the two miles from town?"

Elna soon had dinner on the table, and she and Hans began feeling out this young man. They asked about the farm up in Fergus Falls, about Elof's family, and tried to open up a conversation that would tell them what Mary's future might be if she chose to be courted. Elof replied to their questions easily enough, but he was not good at small talk, and he was wondering just how to go about talking with this girl he had come to see. The laughing eyes of her younger sister did not help him much as he tried to concentrate on what the Rings were saying.

Following coffee, the parents made polite conversation for a short while longer and then discreetly withdrew to another room. Not so, Christina. She was enjoying this and intended to play the tormenting teenager role to the hilt. Mary was a quiet girl, and both she and Elof were so shy that they sat there tongue-tied; neither had any idea of how to start the conversation. Christina teased both of them mercilessly.

Elof, for all his shyness and tongue-tied manner, returned home head over heels in love—but not with the girl he had gone to see. Over the next year, a courtship developed between Elof and the vivacious younger sister. Mary later did get married to Henry Stevens, who became chief of police in the town of Wilmar. But in March 1880, Grove City's little Baptist congregation witnessed the marriage of Elof and Christina. They were to live together happily for fifty-seven years, and they became my grandparents.

# Chapter 3

# Edwin

*Edwin was, by five years, the youngest of the Dahlberg family. He was fortunate to have parents who valued education and to have mentors at key points in his life.*

Elof and Christina's two-hundred-acre farm became one of the most beautiful in Ottertail County. It was situated a couple of miles south of Fergus Falls, its house on a knoll overlooking a lake; Elof's brother August and his wife were on the farm adjoining. Elof and Christina started a grove and windbreak, planting five thousand young trees that first spring and sowing rutabaga seed between the rows to keep down the weeds. They harvested two hundred bushels of prime rutabagas in the fall. The following year, they put in four thousand more trees, ash and spruce, on two acres east of the house. They bought two hundred more acres, drained a slough, and planted wheat. It was the richest land on the farm.

Charlie had by this time moved on to Oregon, but Anna and her husband, Sven Hellander, whom she had met on the boat to America, still lived in the area. Nils and Johanna made their home with Elof's family. And a family Elof soon had.

Irene was born in 1881, Arnold in 1882, and a second daughter, Effie, in 1885. The following year, their house was destroyed by fire. It could have been a disaster for the young family, for there was only five hundred dollars of insurance on the house, but the harvested crops and granary were saved. Elof built a temporary house, not much more than a small log cabin, really, to shelter them through the winter, and the following spring he built a new farmhouse. Their fourth child, Henry, was born that September, and yet another son, Edwin, in 1890.

Life could be harsh in the early years despite the abundant crops yielded by the rich Minnesota soil. Of all the hardships—blizzards, fires, grasshoppers, and isolation among them—illness was one of the most daunting. Johanna never had recovered her hearing after the fever of her first year on the farm. Medical skills were rudimentary even in the cities, and doctors were not always available in the frontier towns. There were no antibiotics. Although America already had four medical schools by the beginning of the nineteenth century, the first school to teach the basics of modern medicine, as the twentieth century understands them, was still more than a decade in the future when Christina's children were small. Thus, when little Edwin became ill with a fever one day, there was not much that could be done.

Christina held him in her arms, walked the floor, and crooned lullabies as he cried fretfully. She watched, fearfully, as he refused food, holding his neck stiffly back as if to ease the muscle spasms. Sponging his forehead seemed to bring no relief. Eleven-year-old Irene would carry him to allow her mother a few hours of rest, but when Christina took him back, he seemed, if anything, much worse. Only his head and torso were feverish now, his limbs cold and limp. His eyes were dull, half-closed. He did not seem so stiff anymore, but he wouldn't drink even with his mother's urging, and he hadn't wet all day. There was a faint blue cast around his mouth, and his breathing became slower and less regular. The parents bent over his crib, silently praying, watching as the little chest became motionless. Then heaved a few more times. Then stopped again. Then made a few feebler efforts. Then stopped.

Little Edwin's death from meningitis was a devastating blow.[1] Elof and Christina felt that their arms would always remain empty. Elof submitted the obituary to the *Fergus Falls Weekly Mail*: "This is to announce to our relatives and friends that Jesus, the friend of little children, has taken home to himself our youngest son, Edwin Theodore, Saturday, the 6th of February, at the age of one year, one month, and twenty days. He is mourned by us his parents, and by his brothers and sisters."

> *Sof i ro, du lilla Edwin,*          Sleep in peace, dear little Edwin,
> *Du ar sa i godt forvar.*            You are now in safest keeping.
> *Hos var Jesus mots vi ater*         For when we meet with Jesus Christ,
> *Doden skiljer oss ej der;*          Not even death shall part us anymore.
> *Du liksom en Noah's dufva*          Just as the dove from the ark of Noah
> *Fann ej plats pa denna jord,*       Found no rest upon the earth,
> *Du till arken flog i frid*          So you have turned again to the ark
> *Undan lifvets sorg och strid.*      From the flood of life and sorrow.[2]

> —*Christina och E. Dahlberg*

Elof and Christina were overjoyed at the birth of another son on 27 December of that same year, 1892. It was not uncommon, in Swedish custom, to give the new child the name of the one that had been lost. So this baby was also named Edwin Theodore, and the previous baby was ever after known as Edwin-that-died. When her youngest son was in his fifties, Christina told him that if his brother had not died, he probably would not have been born. He would often have the feeling that, in many ways, he was living his brother's life for him.[3]

## Early Life on the Farm

Although there were many neighboring farms in Ottertail County in the 1890s, a boy's horizons in those days were mostly limited to the distance he could walk. Even the town of Fergus Falls, two miles to the north, was a different world. The Dahlberg children helped with the farm chores; Henry earned ten cents a week watching the cattle on free-land prairie, a tedious job. Edwin helped keep the gophers at bay. Their holes and mounds caused a lot of trouble for the hay mowers. Elof paid five cents apiece for pocket gophers. Gray gophers brought three cents, and the less bothersome striped gophers a penny. The boys would pour water down the gopher hole and snare the gopher as it came out.

But the children's memories centered mainly on school. All five of them were bright, and all eventually went on to college, but they started out in one room, where all eight grades (totaling nine pupils) met together. In the winter, the schoolteacher, Miss Ada Zendt, would come flying across the prairie in a cutter drawn by two Shetland ponies. She opened the building, heated it, cleaned it, and taught all eight grades with much personal attention to each pupil. Edwin started in the first grade at age four, not only because he could do it, but probably also because his mother was glad, by that time, to get all the children out from under foot.

When he was eight going on nine, Edwin, together with thirteen-year-old Henry and sixteen-year-old Effie, transferred to the school in Fergus Falls. He hated it; not only were there now forty pupils to a room, but the games at recess were different. At the one-room school, they had played duck-on-a-rock and Annie-Annie-over. The town kids played baseball, football, run-sheep-run, and other games that he did not know. He would stand with his back to the wall and was so lonely that he felt sick. Moreover, the school principal felt that the proper place for an eight-year-old was third grade, not fifth, and Edwin was demoted. It was not until his big sister persuaded the principal to test him in reading, spelling, and arithmetic, all of which tests he passed, that his fifth-grade standing was restored.

The three children stayed in town during the week, living in two small rooms over the grocery store—doing their own cooking and getting their own wood and water. Each Friday afternoon Elof or Christina would pick them up and take them back to the farm; each Sunday evening they were sent back, along with a washtub filled with bread, cookies, beans, and fruit.

Minnesota winters being what they were, the school in town usually closed from December to early March, and the children studied at home. Grandfather Nils, now a widower, lived in his own small house a hundred yards down the path and took his meals with Elof's family. He took over the job of teaching the younger children during winter break, using a little wooden pointer for the words in his Swedish Bible.[4] Nils was fifty-two when he came to America, and he never saw a need to learn English. He did have one English word, "please," which he used mostly as an adjective for anything of which he approved. Despite his marginal grasp of the English language, the Swedish American culture of Fergus Falls gave him a chance to practice his American citizenship, of which he was very proud. Every election day, he voted at the country schoolhouse; he even served on juries.

It was Grandfather Nils's theory that anyone could understand Swedish, if he or she only tried, because it was so *plain*.[5] By the time Edwin was in school, the rest of the family was using English in the home, but he and his grandfather managed to communicate. Edwin later attributed much of his own love of the Bible to the sessions with his grandfather. Grandfather had a Swedish reading book, at the back of which was a picture of a rooster. If Edwin read well, the next day there would be a penny or a piece of candy in the book, which Grandfather assured him had been laid by the rooster.

Grandfather not only taught with a book and a small child on his lap; his grandchildren also learned by watching him. Each evening, when the weather was warmer, Grandfather could be observed sitting on the porch of his little house down the path, quietly praying, softly singing a hymn, and reading his Bible, just as he had done on the original trek from Wilmar to Ottertail County. When he was done, he would put his spectacles in the Bible, get up, and slowly go inside.

Though well into his seventies by this time, Grandfather was still an integral part of the farming operation. Once when Elof and Christina were in Grove City for a state conference of Swedish Baptist churches, the children back on the farm in Fergus Falls awoke to find eight of the cattle dead in the pasture. The dead cows were bloated and swollen, obviously victims of poisoning. Grandfather Nils, his eldest grandson, Arnold, and the hired man spent the whole day skinning them to preserve the hides and burying the carcasses.

The following week after Elof was back, another six cows died in the same way. Arnold got his high-school botany teacher to come out, who sent for another botanist from the state agricultural school down in St. Paul. It turned out that poisonous algae were growing on the lake bottom near the shoreline during the drought that summer. When the cattle came to drink, their hooves pressed out the poisonous juices of the algae into the water they drank. The horses waded out into deeper water to drink and so were not affected. Elof promptly fenced off the lake and built a windmill and stock tank to take the place of the old wooden-handled pump.[6]

## Family Religious Life

Although there was a spirit of devotion in the Dahlberg home, there was no set period of family worship. God was thanked for every meal, but personally and in silence. There was little mention of personal religion in the family circle. Farm work was exhausting for both parents, and not much time was spent on religious training.

The surrounding farm community shared much in customs and worship. Most were Swedish immigrants, and many attended the same Baptist church. Edwin's classmates in school were also his companions in Sunday school. On Sunday afternoons, several families would share the noon meal together, after which the children were free to play, without much restriction in their Sunday recreation. Edwin remembered such times with pleasure, yet acknowledged that there was much of frontier church life that was stern and sometimes artificial. He recalled a Fourth of July picnic when the children were hushed while a visiting dignitary preached for two hours. They had been shooting firecrackers and cap pistols when the speaker shouted, "Am I to preach in the face of such a racket? Either those children stop their noise or I stop preaching!"

The enforcement of adult standards on children's behavior was further illustrated in the receiving of young children at evangelistic meetings. "My brother Henry was fifteen years old, and I ten," recalled Edwin, "when he asked me if I would 'go forward' with him to accept Jesus as

my Savior. We did, and the preacher prayed for me—sincerely, too—but
there was a falseness in my own attitude at that age which I very much
regret. I remember well that all the way home that night, as I rode in the
back seat of the buggy between my mother and the preacher's wife, I tried
to sniffle occasionally, in order that they might think that I was sorry for
my past wickedness. Because of the rattle of the wheels, however, they
did not hear me."

Years later in a paper written in seminary, Edwin evaluated the religious community of his youth: "In many ways, the religious life of the
community was mistaken. Sometimes the preacher would denounce the
people for letting their children speak English instead of Swedish. The
social and athletic programs of the public schools were vigorously condemned, as well as the study of science and language."[7] Edwin's oldest
brother, Arnold, passing directly from this environment into a science
course at the university, became an agnostic for three or four years as a
result of his perplexity over what was taught at college versus at church.
Edwin reflected that he might have gone through the same conflict if the
family had not moved to Minneapolis when he was ten.[8]

Elof and Christina had a great respect for knowledge. Elof only had the
opportunity for an eighth-grade education himself, but he wanted something better for the next generation and served for a while as clerk of the
local school board. Christina had only gone through third grade. Both of
them, however, had two consuming passions for their children: first, that
they might all live godly lives, be faithful Christians and faithful members
of the Christian church; and second, that all five might have a college
education. (Elof's hopes for his three sons were for one to manage the
farm, one to enter business, and one to be a lawyer, but he was satisfied
with the professions they chose.)[9] Accordingly, to make it possible for
them to attend the University of Minnesota, Elof sold the farm in 1903,
getting a good price of about $20,000 for the 420 acres because of the
previous year's bumper crop. He then moved his family to Minneapolis.[10]

## Life in the City

The Dahlbergs were uncomfortable in their new environment at first. On
the first Sunday in their new home, they went to the nearest Baptist
church. Tanned by the wind and sun, ill at ease in the first English-speaking church they had ever attended—the university church at that—they
felt like an odd-looking group of Swedish country cousins adrift in the

big city. But they were immediately made welcome by a Scottish couple, the Smiths, who came to call that very afternoon and invited them to join the church. Hugh Smith was a construction foreman and a deacon in the church, with a Scottish accent "so rough you could have sharpened a scythe with it." They probably would have joined anyway, but it was nice to be welcomed, not only that first day, but to feel welcome as the weeks went on.[11]

Edwin got a new viewpoint at Olivet Baptist Church in Minneapolis. It was only two blocks from the University of Minnesota, and he saw college men and women taking the lead in the life of the church, in contrast to the church back by the farm where higher education had been condemned. The youth group was made up almost entirely of high school and university students, and he and several other small boys liked to mingle with them, sneaking into as many mass meetings and football games as they could.[12]

School was another story for Edwin. He would have entered the seventh grade that fall at the age of ten, but once more was put back, this time into the fifth. His sister Effie again intervened, persuading the principal to test him, and he was allowed into the seventh. His own experiences made him sympathetic in later life to children of migrant workers and military personnel, who must adjust to new schools every year or two. In addition to his schoolwork, Edwin had an afternoon paper route with the *Minneapolis Tribune* when he was in high school, building the route to 175 customers. He admitted getting a zero in one algebra test, but in general he was an excellent student. At the age of sixteen, he graduated as valedictorian of East High School's class of 1909.

## Stirrings of a Call

Edwin Dahlberg's life was pointed in a new direction by the pastor who came to the church when Edwin was fourteen. Rutledge Wiltbank was distant and reserved with adults but had a particular affinity for the young people in his church. He could drop-kick a football, and he could hit a baseball so far into the woods that it was never found. He knew how to have fun, but he also could demand reverence in church worship and get it. Edwin regarded him as the ideal pastor.

Wiltbank was visiting the Dahlberg home one afternoon and asked the fourteen-year-old boy casually, "Edwin, what are you going to be when you grow up?"

"I'm not sure yet," he answered, "but I'm thinking most of becoming either a newspaper man or a chemist."

"Did you ever think of the Christian ministry?"

"No, I haven't."

"Well, think about it," said the pastor. That was all. There was no pressure from him, nor from Edwin's parents. But one Sunday night two years later, when Edwin was a high-school senior, Mr. Wiltbank preached a sermon on "Why Young Men Should Go into the Ministry." In later years, Edwin didn't recall a thing that the pastor said that night but remembers saying to a girlfriend while walking home from church, "What Mr. Wiltbank said in his sermon tonight set me to thinking. Maybe I might go into the ministry." Her comment was encouraging: "I think maybe you should."[13]

But after graduating from high school at sixteen years of age, Edwin did not yet feel ready for college. He wanted to earn some money and wanted to see a bit of the world first. His brother Henry had a job in a sugar beet refinery in Spreckels, California, and that looked like a good place to start. Edwin went off to visit his older sister Irene, who was now living in Seattle, and then took the train for California. He had little concept of the distance involved. He ate the sandwiches that Irene had packed and went to sleep, only to look out the next morning and learn, from a signpost by the track, that he still had five hundred miles to go.

Edwin got a job in the sugar factory, first as a common laborer, then as a bench chemist in the laboratory, testing the sugar content of beet juices, syrups, and molasses. His monthly wage was four twenty-dollar gold pieces. Spreckels was a factory town with a population of five hundred; the company owned every house. The factory workers were a rough lot, but "grand, big-hearted men," from many parts of the world. Edwin later thought his time with them during this tremendous experience was one of the best preparations for the ministry he could possibly have had.[14]

There was no church or Sunday school in Spreckels, but Edwin thought he could handle a boys' Sunday school class. He collected eight boys between the ages of ten and twelve. "We gathered in a school room where the bell rope hung almost to the floor, and when those youngsters got out of hand, everybody in town knew about it."[15]

There were other interests, too. One of his high-school girlfriends had moved to Wenatchee, Washington, and he resolved to stop there for a visit on his way home to Minnesota in the summer of 1910. One of his coworkers, Henri Nepven, who had moved on to seek work in San

Francisco, twitted him about it in a letter: "Now Ed, I was just delighted to know that the fair lady far away in beautiful Wenatchee is still
thinking about you and that you are still thinking about her, and both
growing taller and bigger every day! [Edwin was seventeen.] So you are
going to see for yourself in August: Look out, or you may lose your eye-
sight!"[16]

After returning to Minneapolis, Edwin had pretty well put the ministry
out of his mind, leaning more and more toward a career in journalism.
But when he entered the university, he began teaching a Sunday school
class of high-school boys and became interested in the activities of the
campus YMCA (Young Men's Christian Association). Slowly, a quiet
conviction began forming in his heart that he would enjoy religious work
and that maybe his particular talents and his desire to serve Christ would
qualify him for such work.

There were talents that he did not have—he was the first to admit that he
had no bent whatsoever for machinery or repairs, and he did not follow his
two brothers into agricultural chemistry. But he recognized that he could
listen to almost anyone and understand that person's viewpoint—where the
person was coming from, as young people would say nowadays—and he
had an integrity that would always seek to understand the truth. Edwin
thought the world and God could use a man with those qualities.

One night Edwin told Pastor Wiltbank, "I think my mind is made up. I
have decided to follow your example and go into the ministry."

Wiltbank was delighted. He immediately invited Edwin over to his
bachelor apartment the next evening, where they talked long into the
night. "If you are going to be a minister," Wiltbank said, "there are two
things you should consider. One is your Christian faith. That comes first
and is the foundation of everything. The other is scholarship. Get the best
theological education. Study a great deal of biography, too, in order to get
a view of history in terms of human personality. Read Alexander V. G.
Allen's *Life of Phillips Brooks* and read as much as you can of Joseph
Addison's essays, for the cultivating of literary style."[17]

Edwin was always grateful for his pastor's advice: "He did not roman-
ticize the ministry or make it some sentimental thing. He put the emphasis where it belonged, on fidelity to Christ, love for people, and on those
intellectual disciplines which along with faith and character are so vital a
factor in the Christian ministry today. He was a broad-minded, liberal
thinker, who did much to spare me from the theological doubts and

wrestlings in which many students become involved, by reason of the seeming conflicts of science, and philosophy, and religion which are not really necessary conflicts at all."[18] Wiltbank also added more concrete help, in the form of a large number of books on science, theology, and preaching from his own professional library to get Edwin started.

In high school, Edwin had never thought much about religion, though he went to church and said his prayers. He had had trouble defining his faith and was uncomfortable in church meetings where the topic was something like "Why I Am a Christian" or "What It Means to Be a Baptist." Such phrases as "being saved" or "being washed in the blood" had no meaning for him in those years; he did not yet understand the process of Christ's taking away his sins. He got some added understanding from attending a study group in his freshman year in college, but he still could not see what Christ had accomplished on the cross. About this time, he began to have long conversations with his oldest sister, Irene, who had recently returned home after becoming widowed at the age of thirty. They recalled a sermon by Pastor Wiltbank in which he said that we should not think so much about the death of Christ that we forget his life. In later years, Edwin admitted that in emphasizing this as a college sophomore he went too far and threw out the crucifixion as having no meaning whatever. "I was a little boastfully liberal," he recalled, "jumping to the conclusion that any preacher that talked about the crucifixion was dealing in old, outworn ideas." Even during this period, however, he never lost faith in God, nor was his high-school decision to enter the ministry ever shaken. His doubts gradually receded during his senior year in college, for which he credits the influence of his family and the discussions they would have on Christ, prayer, and immortality. At this stage, his mother and oldest sister were, as he put it, "outspokenly radical," while his father took a conservative viewpoint.[19]

It was at this time that tragedy again struck his sister. Irene had two children, a son Lorimer, age fourteen, and a daughter Marion, age seven. Lorimer went swimming in Lake Calhoun in Minneapolis with some friends one day and failed to come home. The lifeguard's routine pre-closing check of all the clothes lockers found one with clothes still in it. A search of the lake was then carried out; they finally found Lorimer's body and brought it out of the water at 2 A.M. This was one of Edwin's first encounters with human death—Lorimer was only six years younger than himself—and one of the factors enabling him to empathize with other people's losses later during his professional life.

Edwin's brother Henry, with whom he had worked in the Spreckels, California, sugar refinery, went on to enter the field of sugar chemistry as a lifelong profession. In 1912, Henry's company sent him to Berlin, Germany, for six months to study the advances that were being made in that field, and he invited his brother to go along. Edwin was a college sophomore at Minnesota at the time, but his professors encouraged him to go, allowing him college credit for the experience provided he wrote some papers on his observations and conclusions when he returned. The two young men arrived in Germany as the clouds of World War I were gathering, but international relationships were officially still cordial, and they gained a new international perspective from their time abroad. They also toured Sweden, seeking their family roots in Småland and Skåne and striking up acquaintanceship with third cousins who had remained in the old country.[20]

As Edwin became more self-confident in his college years, and as his philosophical and religious beliefs developed and matured, he became eager to communicate what he felt, and he found that he could hold the attention of any group to which he spoke. His own scholarship led him to examine all sides of a question and look for answers. He majored in public speaking and debate and became part of the university's debate team that toured the small towns of Minnesota in the spring of 1913. Some of his debate-team notes are still preserved in his papers.

The four-member team was assigned the job of debating socialism, pro and con, a hot topic four years before the takeover of Russia by the Bolsheviks. Edwin's opening paragraph, likening socialism to a mirage luring a desert traveler off the road and into the wilderness, bears a professor's comment, "Well done!" After enumerating four fundamental objections to socialist philosophy and discussing the problems with which socialism would have to deal (among them, "Government job examinations may test a man who sails the Mediterranean, but not the Columbus who embarks on a new sea"), Edwin's presentation concludes, "Socialism has the same disease that has weakened us. . . . You can't by magic change a man's heart just by bringing in a new economic system!"[21] The company-owned towns of the Minnesota Iron Range would have none of this discussion, either pro or con, on such a dangerous political subject, and the debate team was required to substitute an evening of less controversial entertainment. The team did, but the members were unhappy about the restriction.

## Seminary Years in Rochester

After graduating from the University of Minnesota in 1914, Edwin planned to attend Chicago Baptist Divinity School, but Pastor Wiltbank, counseling him that he had already had part of his education in the Midwest, recommended his own alma mater at Rochester, New York, later to become Colgate Rochester Divinity School. Here, he met another man who had a major part in shaping his thinking and career.

Walter Rauschenbusch was a professor who had had, in his own early career, a ministry in one of New York City's most infamous slum neighborhoods, known as Hell's Kitchen. He became deeply involved in the lives of those caught in that whirlpool of violence, crime, failed lives, and despair. Rauschenbusch became convinced that an effective minister of the gospel must not only seek the soul of the individual who had lost touch with God but must also address the environment that had led the individual away from God in the first place. Most churchgoers would have agreed with this up to a point—liquor, drugs, illicit sex, and other such temptations were often-cited causes of "going astray." But Rauschenbusch went further. High profits at the expense of low wages, slumlords who failed to maintain New York tenements, wars that drained the assets of whole nations, the industry that produced the liquor, all these and more were proper topics to be addressed by the Christian ministry. "Evangelism and social action go together or you don't have the Gospel!"[22] was his constant theme, and this scraped the nerves of some who did not like to be thus disturbed. In addition, just as some preachers stuck to "saving souls," some others believed that the kingdom of God could be ushered in simply by correcting social evils and working for a social utopia. Rauschenbusch's belief that both approaches must be integral parts of any effective ministry was lost in a rising storm of argument and mutual scorn between "fundamentalist Christians" and "liberal Christians" over the meaning—and desirability—of the "social gospel."

Walter Rauschenbusch was a popular lecturer and an exacting critic of his students' performance. When he thought one of Dahlberg's papers was too effusive and poorly thought out one day, he sent it back with a single comment in the margin: "Cock-a-doodle-doo!"[23]

As it happened, Rauschenbusch was almost totally deaf. He therefore employed one of the seminary students each year to be his "ears" as he taught and lectured. Edwin Dahlberg's grades at the seminary were very good, as they had been at Minnesota, and for his last two years at Rochester he obtained the post of Dr. Rauschenbusch's secretary. At lectures, Edwin would sit inconspicuously at a small table, taking notes in a special shorthand, which Dr. Rauschenbusch read over his shoulder. Rauschenbusch was thus able to reply to the question from the audience almost as fast as if he had heard it himself.

If there was any one person who became Edwin Dahlberg's mentor, it was Rauschenbusch. He impressed his young secretary not only with his lectures but with his personal Christian life. In one week alone, Dahlberg transcribed letters to President Woodrow Wilson, to Prime Minister Lloyd George of England, to a Sunday school teacher out West who asked for help with a question that had come up in her class, and to a little girl in Australia who had written Rauschenbusch about the death of her dog.[24]

Rauschenbusch could hold both the I.W.W. [the International Workers of the World was a radical-left labor union of the times] and the Chamber of Commerce in the palm of his hand, observed Dahlberg. Not only that, but the professor paid great attention to little details, such as counting the number of curbstones over which a mother would have to lift her baby carriage to get her children from the tenement to the nearest public park in the slum neighborhoods.[25]

Rauschenbusch responded to the needs of everyone. At one point earlier in his ministry, his own home had been burglarized by a thief who stole a set of china plates. The police had apprehended the burglar and phoned Dr. Rauschenbusch to come down to the police station to press charges. When he arrived and saw the ragged man who had done the crime, he asked that the man be released into his custody, which was arranged. Over the following weeks and months, Rauschenbusch not only counseled the man but helped him get back on his feet. One evening, he invited the man to dinner at his home, and they ate off the very dishes the man had once stolen. One of the impressions that Edwin Dahlberg carried away from his years as secretary was the ex-burglar's visit to class at the seminary, telling how he had come to accept Christ in his own life through Dr. Rauschenbusch's ministry.[26]

And anxious to have his students see more than one aspect of life, Rauschenbusch also paid the expenses of an ex-safecracker to come lecture his class on the man's conversion to Christianity after stopping at one of evangelist Billy Sunday's meetings while on his way to rob a bank.[27]

## Pacifist Convictions

These years were a time of testing in Edwin Dahlberg's life. While in seminary he developed a firm conviction that war was wrong. He tells the story in a letter many years later:

> During my college days at the University of Minnesota, I was by no means a pacifist. Quite the contrary! According to the rules of the University we were required to take two years of military training. I loved every aspect of it— marching in parade behind our University of Minnesota band, the two weeks we used to spend as freshmen and sophomores, engaged in sentry duty at near-by Fort Snelling; rifle practice also, and sham battles with the National Guard, as we defended the western end of the bridge across the Mississippi River, while the National Guard defended the eastern end. Moreover, we had lectures from time to time by an army colonel, who would speak to us about our duty to be prepared. . . . The patriotic spirit was running like a high fever all over the country, and I was caught up in it completely.
>
> But this was all changed when I entered the Baptist seminary in Rochester, New York. There I came under the influence of Walter Rauschenbusch, my professor of church history. He was the greatest person I have ever known. He had been greatly saddened by the war. He had one nephew in the French army and another nephew in the German army. This just about broke his heart, and I think was a big factor in bringing about his death when he was at the very height of his career.[28]

"I am not sure that [Rauschenbusch] was completely a pacifist himself," continued Dahlberg in retelling the events later, "but he was one of the very first to recognize the folly of World War I, 'the war to end all war,' supposedly. . . . None of my professors [at Minnesota], fine as they were, had the foresight to sense what Walter Rauschenbusch foresaw, so far as I know. He was a prophet ahead of his time. The rest of us were all caught up in the war spirit, I among the rest of them. Many of my classmates in the class of 1914 responded to their country's call, and died in that war."[29]

The more he listened to Rauschenbusch, the more Dahlberg was convinced that he himself must become a conscientious objector and resist the war. In the spring of 1917, fifteen students met to discuss what stand they should take. The meeting was a communion service, held in the dormitory room of Dahlberg and his roommate, Harlan Frost, and presided over by Dr. Henry B. Robins, chairman of the department of missions. In that discussion, the fifteen agreed that each should choose his own means of opposition to war. All were entitled to draft deferment as theological students or clergy, but they felt it necessary to express their stand in stronger terms. Some chose the army chaplaincy; some, the ambulance service or the YMCA canteen program. Others, including Dahlberg, felt that a pacifist could not honestly participate in any form of war service sponsored by the military.

Dahlberg recognized the reality of war; during his career he was pastor to hundreds of young soldiers and always ministered to their needs without trying to place any personal guilt on those who chose to fight for their country. Indeed, he was to gain the respect of military officers for his visits at Christmastime to military outposts all over the world, but by personal conviction he was a pacifist, a conscientious objector to war—all war.

In 1917 this was not at all a popular attitude. America was about to enter the war, and the draft law was in effect. To him, draft deferment as a theological student was sidestepping the issue. He believed that war was wrong and that the matter must be faced head on; he was not afraid of the consequences.

Dahlberg's seminary class graduated in 1917. He had been accepted for a year of postgraduate study and spent the summer working on his brother Arnold's farm in northern Minnesota. One late afternoon at milking time, a neighbor stopped by and introduced himself as the chairman of the county draft board. He said the draft-board office had closed for the day, but he thought he would stop by and pick up some of the registrations on his way home. "I don't think I have yours yet," he said. Edwin thanked him for coming, but said he was not planning to register. The neighbor was astonished. "But you've got to register. It's the law!"

"I know that. But I don't believe in the war, and I can't conscientiously register for the draft."

The man left, puzzled. Nothing further happened for several weeks, except that Dahlberg heard a new word in the neighborhood, "slacker." Then late one afternoon, he and Arnold were fencing the pasture, pounding in fence posts with a sixteen-pound sledgehammer and stretching barbed wire from post to post. He saw an old Ford driving down the fence row. A big man in a ten-gallon hat got out and talked to Arnold awhile, then came over to Edwin and pleasantly introduced himself as the sheriff of Marshall County. "I've been going around the county the past few weeks picking up the draft registrations that haven't come in yet, so I thought I would come over and get yours this afternoon. You can sign up right here. I'll see that it's turned in to the county office."

Dahlberg explained the reasons why he felt he could not sign up, being a conscientious objector. The sheriff listened patiently awhile and then said, "Do you really insist on carrying out your idea of resisting the draft?" When Dahlberg said that he did, the sheriff showed his badge, laid a heavy hand on Dahlberg's shoulder, and said, "Then it becomes my duty to place you under arrest." He got out a pair of handcuffs.

"That's not really necessary, Sheriff," said Edwin's brother. "The boy isn't going to try to escape."

"Well, what do you think I ought to do, Arnold?" asked the sheriff.

"Why don't you come up to the house for supper, and we'll talk about it," suggested Arnold. "My father and mother are here too. We'll just tell them that you're a friend who stopped in." The sheriff accepted the invitation and was introduced to Elof and Christina (who were visiting from Minneapolis) as a Liberty Bond salesman, which was true.

But that night, Edwin's mother came to his room. "Wasn't that the sheriff, here to dinner? What did he want?" When she learned that it was not just a casual visit, she wept. "Oh, Edwin, please register for the draft. If you don't, we will all be disgraced, and it will be so hard for you." Her weeping was difficult to resist, but he said that he had taken his stand against the war and was firm in his purpose to continue. After more pleading, she kissed him good night and went wearily to bed.

Edwin recalled in later years, "When I continued my refusal to register for the draft, I was deeply moved by the way my entire family went into action in their efforts to help me. They did not agree with my position, but how they rallied around me. My fiancée, Emilie Loeffler [who had two brothers in the Allied Expeditionary Force in France], wrote to me that she would stand by me, whatever happened, although she did not fully agree with me." His brother Henry came to St. Paul from Denver to talk with the lieutenant governor but was told, "If this is still his position, there is only one answer. Either he will go to the prison at Joliet, Illinois, or to the federal prison at Fort Leavenworth, Kansas."

A few days later, Edwin's mother had a heart attack, and his father had to call the doctor. Whether it was a true coronary or a violent emotional reaction is uncertain. It staggered Edwin as nothing up till that time had.

That is the hardest part of holding to any conviction [Edwin said years later], the wounding of those you love. I can remember as though it were yesterday, that beautiful morning in 1917 when my father and I sat down on a log together out in the woods, on my brother's farm, to talk things over. He pleaded

with me to change my attitude. He reminded me of the heartache my position
was causing the whole family circle. He was worried for fear I would never
receive a call to the pastorate of a church. In later years, after seeing more fully
the folly and futility of the wars that were supposed to make the world safe for
democracy, he understood my convictions better, and in a measure, began to
share them. But I shall never forget the weariness with which he got up from
the log on that long-ago morning, walking away though the woods with his
white head bowed in sorrow and discouragement. He was so patient, so kind.[30]

Seeing what his stand was doing to his parents, Edwin realized that
whatever path he chose, there would be something both right and wrong
about it. He felt thoroughly shaken, not knowing how to handle the situation, or even how to handle life itself. Later that day, he told his parents
that he would register, as a conscientious objector. He felt a strong sense
of guilt that he was being untrue not only to himself but to Jesus Christ.
A sense of unworthiness was to burden him for years afterward. It was
not until the beginning of World War II—when he told the whole story in
a sermon—that he felt the burden lift.

Interviewed by L. Doward McBain years later, Dahlberg recalled:
"Though each of us fifteen chose his own method, each kept his promise
not to bear arms nor to kill his fellow men. One or two were placed under
technical arrest, and some of us were looked down upon as being obstruc-
tionists of government. Though the protest wasn't very successful, I think
each of us came closer to the cross of Christ than in all of the theology
classes we attended. What's more, I think we were right."

## Ordination

At the end of Dahlberg's four years at Rochester, which he passed with
high grades, the time came for ordination. This is a ceremony officially
recognizing the call to God's ministry, a sort of passing the mantle from
older experienced pastors to the young. Among Baptists, it usually takes
place at the candidate's home church. The ceremony is preceded by an
ordination council at which ministers of the area are free to question in a
public meeting the young aspirant's calling, abilities, and beliefs.
Especially the beliefs. One council member's disputation of the candidate's theology is enough to hold up the whole process. The council may
suggest that the candidate "pray about it some more," a euphemism for
postponing the ordination.

As might be expected, conservative Minnesota had a number of ministers whose theology did not reach consensus with the teaching of schools back East, and Edwin Dahlberg's ordination was postponed three times. On one occasion Edwin's mother, sitting among the spectators, stood up to declare to the august council, in her usual outspoken manner, "I don't know anything about theology, but Edwin is a good boy!"[31]

Amid smiles at this interruption, maybe some of the council members recalled that the examination's purpose was to decide the competence of this young man, not debate esoteric points of theology among themselves. In any case, Edwin eventually was ordained a minister of the gospel. He kneeled for the traditional laying on of hands, while all the ministers present placed their hands on his bowed head and prayed that God's Spirit would empower his ministry. In the summer of 1918, he was ready to begin work.

# Chapter 4

# Pastor

*Professional success depends not only on the opportunities and challenges along the path but on one's priorities in responding. Edwin T. Dahlberg was aware of his responsibility to God, to the individuals to whom he ministered, to the community, and to his family. All were important. If something was in God's plan, it was, by definition, possible.*

Rochester Theological Seminary had not only given Edwin Dahlberg a solid grounding in scholarship, theology, and preaching; it had also, inadvertently, provided him with a wife. Emilie Louise Loeffler, age twenty-three, daughter of a Rochester lithographer, had caught Edwin's eye at an afternoon reception, and he soon began courting her. They became engaged in the spring of 1917.

Edwin preserved his fiancée's letters written when they were apart during the summers of 1917, when he was working on his brother's farm in Minnesota, and 1918 , when he was beginning his first pastorate in northern New York. The fifth of seven children in the Loeffler family, Emilie was a volunteer at the Lake Avenue Baptist Church of Rochester where she supervised a teenage Christian Endeavor class and arranged for replacement teachers for the Sunday school. She cooked for the family and evidently defended herself against her two younger brothers' good-natured teasing about writing letters to her fiancé. Her letters in 1917 expressed her anxiety about the possibility of Edwin spending a year in jail for his beliefs. She agreed with his pacifist stand but urged him to reconsider his vow not to register for the draft. Always the letters expressed how much she missed him.[1]

Few details of the courtship are recorded, except for the afternoon when Edwin steeled himself to approach her father to ask for her hand in marriage. Charles Loeffler knew the purpose of the young man's call perfectly well, but he let the tension build a bit. He insisted on taking Edwin on a tour of the entire lithography plant, explaining the printing process in detail. Edwin tried to appear interested, but his mind was elsewhere. When he could finally introduce the topic for which he had come, Charles—who had already decided that the young man would be a satisfactory husband for his daughter—agreed to the request unhesitatingly. On 27 August 1918, two months after Edwin finished seminary, he and Emilie were married.

## Potsdam, New York, 1918

As early as his second year at seminary, Edwin had begun exploring job opportunities. In 1917, he was offered a job at the Baptist Publication Society but decided instead to take a chance on a scholarship for a year of postgraduate study (which he received). He asked about work in the YMCA but was told they were only hiring men above the draft age. He worked weekends in his postgraduate year as a supply pastor to several small rural churches and found that he enjoyed "country work." He offered himself to the candidate committee of a small church in the far north of New York State, First Baptist Church of Potsdam. Young seminary graduates do not get the big churches.

Potsdam had a population of 4,500 people, plus another 1,000 at Clarkston College. The church's membership in the previous fifteen years had dropped from 184 to 112, but there were two satellite congregations at South Colton and Stark, which added perhaps 55 members to the total. Potsdam offered a salary of $1,100 per year ($300 of it a subsidy from the New York State Baptist office). The church would supply a house with a new hot-air furnace, both hot and cold water, and electric lights.

In 1918, as in the 1990s, church committees examined candidates closely, especially their politics and theology. St. Lawrence County was conservative enough to have voted "dry" even before Prohibition was added to the U.S. Constitution, and they did not want to get some radical in the pulpit. How did he view the war? The candidate replied, "President Wilson's war aims [Dahlberg's diplomatically chosen phrase for President Wilson's hopes for a League of Nations] express the true spirit of the American people. But the present war and Christianity are not identical."[2] And socialism? Dahlberg replied that he was against division of property but in favor of labor getting a larger share in running industry and a larger share of profits. He realized that it would not happen overnight. Where did he stand on Bolshevism, then? Dahlberg agreed that Bolshevism (Communism) is a menace to the United States, though not all U.S. organizations that are labeled Bolshevik really are. He commended investigation and correction of labor complaints.[3] What was his stand on the second coming of Christ? Dahlberg replied, "There are different views of the second coming, all Biblical. I believe it will be gradual, as the world comes into obedience with Christ's teachings; [the apostle] Paul believed it would be sudden. . . . We won't find complete agreement between all parts of the Bible . . . because the men God used to write it lived in different centuries and in as different conditions as today versus [the era] of the American Indian."[4]

Pulpit committees seldom are effusive about a new candidate, but they evidently decided the young man would do. Dahlberg got the post, and he and his new bride moved in. It was that first year in Potsdam that the great influenza pandemic struck, killing twenty-one million people worldwide. Emilie caught it, and there was some concern that it would affect the pregnancy she had just started, but their first child, Margaret Emilie, was born without difficulty the next July in the hospital at nearby Ogdensburg.

Being pastor to three small congregations meant traveling forty-eight miles of dirt road every Sunday, preaching four times, and overseeing the Sunday school and the youth group, as well as conducting weddings and funerals and assisting attempts to patch up broken marriages and dysfunctional families. In such manner, a young minister builds up experience and ability.

Dahlberg credits one experience in Potsdam with influencing his ministry more than he realized at the time. It was, of course, the Prohibition era in postwar America, and Potsdam was not far from the Canadian border, where illegal liquor was smuggled into the country. At the invitation of a couple of federal agents, he and a young Presbyterian minister went along one night as spectators in a raid on a speakeasy (illegal tavern):

> In what was quite a cloak and dagger adventure, we crawled up a back stairway with the federal men into a dark attic, jumped down through a trapdoor into the room below where we took half a dozen men completely by surprise. Pointing to one of the men, the federal agent shouted, "Arrest that man on an open charge!" Instantly the liquor seller smashed a bottle of whiskey into the sink, destroying the evidence. One of the federal men gathered up what evidence he could, and then we all proceeded to the police station, where two of the rumrunners were booked for possession and sale of illegal liquor.
>
> As I saw the two men handcuffed to their chairs, sullen in the one case and discouraged in the other, a vast feeling of revulsion swept over me. There came to me the words of Jesus, when quoting from the prophet Isaiah, he said, "The Spirit of the Lord is upon me, because he has anointed me to preach the gospel

to the poor. He has sent me to heal the brokenhearted, to preach deliverance to the captives, and recovery of sight to the blind, to set at liberty them that are bruised" (Luke 4:18).

I suddenly realized that as a minister of the gospel I was stepping out of character. There was need for law and police power. But it was not for me. My responsibility was not to take men captive, but to set them free. So it was that although we got a great many letters of praise in the newspapers for breaking up a rum-running ring, I never went on a police raid again. Instead I have gone to prisons all over the world, from Sing Sing to Brussels, from Tel Aviv in Israel to the refugee camps in Burma, seeking, as did Jesus, to bind up the brokenhearted, to set the prisoner free, "to set at liberty them that are bruised."[5]

This raid, and Rauschenbusch's treatment of his burglar, influenced the young pastor's lifelong attitude toward those in trouble with the law. It was not sentimentality but acceptance of the person, doing what he could to meet the needs of both the prisoner and the prisoner's family. Occasionally, he maintained contact for twenty years or more, long after he had left a particular pastorate.

## Buffalo, New York, 1921

After three years in Potsdam, Edwin Dahlberg had a call to Buffalo to take the pastorate of the Maple Street Baptist Church. For Baptists, the transfer to a new church is a transaction between the church and the candidate; there is no bishop or council involved. The church in need of a new pastor usually appoints several of its members as a pulpit (or search) committee, who will then consider any minister the members know about, perhaps seeking advice from the regional executive minister or from a nearby seminary. After discussing several of the most promising candidates, the committee may visit the candidate's present church to hear the candidate preach and get an idea of what sort of person and what sort of administrator he or she is. (So the sight of a row of unfamiliar faces seated in a single pew generally alerts a minister and arouses the spouse's curiosity.) If the committee members' report to their home church is favorable, the church "issues a call" to the minister, who is free to accept or decline. The minister may feel that he or she has accomplished the hoped-for dreams and goals for the present congregation—or may have concluded that there is little likelihood of ever doing so—and may be ready for a move. Though some ministers choose to stay in a church for several decades, most are ready to go on to new challenges in five to ten years.

Dahlberg had had three years in a rural church and was ready to see what he could do in an urban setting. Maple Street Baptist in Buffalo was not a large church; it was in the inner city in a somewhat run-down area where many low-income families lived. The job offered $2,800 per year, a month's vacation, and moving expenses. The house rent would be $40 per month.

City ministry included aspects and opportunities that were not always a part of work in a small town. The church neighborhood had a large minority of Chinese immigrants who had entered the country just before the Asian Exclusion Act went into effect. In addition to his regular duties, Dahlberg took over teaching the Chinese men's Bible class at the YMCA each Sunday afternoon. Many years later, he was still receiving letters from former class members. Buffalo also had a number of enterprises delicately referred to in those days as "houses." The pastor's work occasionally took him there, but he was always careful to take his wife with him on such calls, explaining to anyone who asked that it was not only important to avoid evil but in certain cases to avoid also the appearance of evil. It would not have occurred to him to disdain anyone who worked in the oldest profession; such women were in need of Jesus' help just as much as anyone else.

His counselling encounters did not always have happy endings. Many involved emotional or mental disturbance, sickness, marital problems, and the like. As in any profession, counselling skill comes through practice, through being available, patient, objective, and considerate. He found a sense of humor helpful, though he expressed it gently. He readily admitted that not every marriage was saved, nor every youngster kept out of jail.

It was during Dahlberg's Buffalo ministry that his two sons were born: Bruce Theodore in 1924, and myself, Keith Ramel, in 1929. (It seems appropriate at this point for me to start referring to him as Dad. Few people called him Edwin T. Dahlberg. To his professional colleagues he was Ed; to his wife, Teddy; to the family at large, Uncle Ted, or Grandpa, as the case might be.)

Maple Street Baptist Church grew to the point at which the old building was no longer adequate, and the congregation voted to start a building campaign. Even in the prosperous late 1920s, $100,000 was a debt not to be assumed lightly by a small- to medium-size church. Dad and Mother felt they could not ask the church members to contribute without making a significant lead-off contribution themselves, even though it meant a financial sacrifice. On Dad's twentieth birthday, his father had given him a $5,000 life-insurance policy. Dad had completed the payments by 1927. He borrowed as much as he could on this, $1,500, to start the building fund, and the church members came through with the funds to build what later was renamed the Masten Park Church. It took years to pay back the loan, but Dad and Mother regarded it as the best investment they ever made.[6]

The young minister gradually acquired a reputation beyond the local church. A sermon at the state youth convention in Albany in 1922 was so well received that Keuka College invited him to preach the closing sermon of its school year the following June. In October of 1923, he was offered the chair of psychology and ethics at Hillsdale College, but he preferred to continue his vocation as a pastor.

During the Buffalo years, Dad was becoming aware of differing viewpoints among his Baptist colleagues, differences that were to involve him in escalating conflict and mediation in years to come. A pastor at Schenectady, New York, wrote him, apparently as a part of a statewide campaign, about the "radical liberals" who were causing trouble in the state Baptist Convention and were threatening to drive the conservative churches into the arms of the more militant anti-Convention fundamentalists. He proposed formation of a new fellowship of middle-of-the-road conservative pastors to preserve the mission work and organization of New York State Baptists.[7]

Dad wrote in reply that, although his own outlook was that of a liberal in theological view and would differ considerably from fundamentalists in interpretation of faith, he counted himself as an earnest and thoroughly evangelistic Baptist and in agreement with the writer's appeal for Baptist unity. But he went on to suggest that the average layperson is bewildered by all the committees and organizations within the church. Rather than forming a new fellowship, he personally favored working through existing Baptist channels to encourage loyalty and mission effort: "The whole question centers around this issue: whether we can be loyal to different interpretations of our Christian faith, and at the same time be loyal to the same Baptist organization. As for myself, I believe this is possible. A great many do not feel so, however, and sooner or later we have to settle this decisive question."[8]

In October of 1931, with the new church building in Buffalo completed and the congregation growing, Dad felt open to accepting a new challenge. He chose to answer a call from back in his home state of Minnesota, to a church that appeared to be in a peculiar, even precarious, position.

## St. Paul, Minnesota, 1931

First Baptist Church of St. Paul, Minnesota, was probably the leading Baptist church not only of St. Paul but of the whole state. Established in 1849, when the future state capital was only a collection of small frame houses, the church had grown along with the city. The present building, when completed in 1875, was said to be the most beautiful church building west of Chicago. It was built of brown native stone with a high, sloping roof and originally had a steeple 165 feet tall. The main room, or sanctuary, had a hushed, calm atmosphere. I remember one particular stained-glass window that pictures dazzlingly yellow sheaves of wheat under a blue prairie sky.

But by the depression years of the 1930s, the surrounding homes of the well-to-do had been sold and turned into rooming houses. The church neighborhood was littered with papers and refuse scattered by the wind; drunks stumbled slowly down the street or slept in doorways. Although perhaps 25 percent of the members were on relief during the 1930s, the church itself had not gone downhill in the usual inner-city scenario. Its members included college professors, blue-collar workers, business professionals, soldiers from Fort Snelling, pensioners, and people who were simply down on their luck, people who lived in all parts of town but who still chose to come downtown to worship.

A deteriorating neighborhood, however, was not First Church's main problem in 1931. Over its eighty-year history, it had had a number of able pastors but now found itself saddled with a man whom some of the congregation held in high regard and whom others thought to be totally incompetent. One member recalls from his own teenage years that the pastor had been caught several times in a lie, that his sermons were constant repetitions, always having the refrain "Pra-a-aise the Lord!" And he remembered the pastor on several different occasions coming into the pulpit and saying something like this: "It's been a very busy week, and I've not had time to prepare a sermon, so I'll just call on you, Deacon Ferguson, to come to the pulpit and just share whatever is on your heart!" Or other times it could be Brother Booth or Our Friend Ed Randall. The more fundamentalist members loved it; they felt that a born-again Christian should be able to stand up at any time and in any place and testify and that everybody should gladly accept it. But some members, particularly among the teachers and business and professional people, were not going to tolerate such a level of competence for very long.[9]

It appeared that the church, for eighty-two years a beacon in the community, would inevitably split, perhaps irreparably. The young member, whose recollections are cited above, recalls the unrelieved tensions in the congregation. He could hardly wait to get to Wednesday night prayer meeting, not because he was pious, but because he knew that every meeting would always end in one glorious fight! People argued about what the church ought to be and would sometimes get into towering rages. Sunday mornings likewise revealed the divisions in the congregation. On the left sat the followers of engraver N. T. Mears, the friend of the head of the fundamentalist faction of the state, and to the right of the pulpit were those led by moderate/conservative lumberman W. C. Stanton. Tensions mounted week by week. Delighted as the young spectator had been to see them vociferously debating the meaning of the Bible in the life and operation of a church, he became sobered as he saw these much-admired people getting more and more solemn and distraught.

The crisis built to a point at which the minister was asked to resign. He did so but took two hundred of the congregation with him and started a new church about a mile away. The local newspapers had been following the conflict avidly. A *St. Paul Times* editorial for 7 February 1931 commented,

> It is hard to understand the ministerial ethics of the gentleman who retired from the First Baptist Church a couple of weeks ago, and availed himself of the generosity of the church to remain on the payroll till April 11th, and immediately attempts to start another church, and assumes the role of "guest preacher," to last while his name is on the payroll of the First Baptist Church. To a common editor, who does not profess a great degree of holiness, that looks like a dirty trick. If he had so little of the attributes of leadership that he could not get along with his congregation, the decent thing for him to do was retire. Just how he can square his conduct with the religious philosophy he has been preaching from his pulpit in the past two and a half years is beyond our ken.[10]

The rival *Pioneer Press* reported the first meeting in the Palm Room of the Hotel St. Paul of the breakaway church members, who had plans for a new building.

The consensus in the city was that if the First Baptist Church could ever get a new pastor, the man was to be pitied.

What the church got was Edwin T. Dahlberg. Hardly anyone had ever heard of him. He was from back East somewhere. What everyone wanted to know was, Is this man Dahlberg, whoever he is, big enough to come into this situation and accomplish anything? Will we ever be a real church again? Certainly, he did not look like much . . . no hearty personality to inspire confidence. He had dignity and restraint and good humor, but could he clear the hostility from the air? (It did not help either, the first Sunday, to see Mrs. Dahlberg and the three children seated on the fundamentalist side of the congregation. But it turned out she was unaware that where one sat in this church made a political statement; she had merely chosen the pew closest to the door that led to her husband's office.)[11]

The enigma in this situation was N. T. Mears, the leader of the fundamentalist faction. He had chosen to stay with the church and indeed was president of the congregation. When he moved to St. Paul in 1914, his friend W. B. Riley, then pastor of the First Baptist Church of Minneapolis, had encouraged him to go down to First Church in St. Paul because he thought they were in need of more spiritual leadership there.[12] Secretary-treasurer of the Buckbee Mears Engraving Company, N. T. hardly looked the spiritual type. His photographs show a stocky man, hat set square on his head, mouth in a firm horizontal line, gazing straight at the camera as though daring it to say something. He was used to being in control. According to one anecdote (maybe apocryphal), he was once hospitalized for pneumonia but grew rebellious at having to stay at rest. He announced his intention to leave the hospital. His family confiscated his car keys. Undaunted, he got dressed, walked across the street to a car dealership, paid cash on the spot for a new car, and drove home.

A clash with the new minister was inevitable. When it came, it was surprisingly quiet and brief. Irate at some point of dissension in a meeting of the board of trustees, N. T. got up and started to walk out. Dad said calmly, "Norman, come back and sit down." And N. T. sat.

Perhaps Mr. Mears had stayed on with the church because he really did want the church to succeed and he now found that the new man maybe had enough gumption to make it happen. He often disagreed with Dad, but Dad didn't mind. At almost weekly Monday sessions, N. T. would try to set the pastor straight on theological matters. Dad would always listen attentively and sometimes agree with N. T.'s point of view and at other times firmly explain why yesterday's sermon was correct just as it was preached. N. T. gradually, by his own account, grew to admire Dad, but he never gave up trying to convert him to his own point of view.

Our family always enjoyed an invitation to the Mearses' home. Mrs. Mears was as grandmotherly as her husband was gruff. The food was good, the conversation interesting even to a small boy, and there was a big barn full of hay to explore with two of the Mears grandchildren, Norman C. and Elwood. Mealtime at the home was a vociferous debate among the members of the Mears family. N. B., one of the sons, was just as much a liberal as his father was a fundamentalist, and several of the older children contributed their own vehement opinions while eating large helpings of fresh food from the family farm.

As other church members came to know their new pastor, many of them, too, gradually began to regain hope. His preaching addressed their concerns and needs; it was easy to follow and interesting besides. He would start by focusing on some spiritual concern, then point out all sides of the question, almost as if to reassure every listener of the understandability of his or her own point of view. He would then go on to develop what was for him the answer.[13]

And always, at the end of the sermon, the announcement of the closing song would include an invitation to anyone who did not yet know Jesus to come forward publicly and acknowledge the intent to follow him. Not tearful, not demanding, not mechanical, the invitation was just offered in a friendly conversational voice: "Now it may be that there is someone here today who has never acknowledged Jesus as his Lord and Savior. If you would like to do that, or if you are already a Christian but would like to unite with this church, why not come forward during the singing of this hymn. People will make way for you, there is no need to feel embarrassed; one of the deacons will be here to talk with you after the end of the service." Such a commonsense approach, including, as it always did, an appeal to trust Jesus' invitation to come to God, not only appealed to the congregation but established the pastor's credibility. Some may have been afraid of the rumor that Dahlberg was a "liberal." If he was, they guessed it did not mean he disbelieved the Bible or disclaimed the need for evangelism.

Not satisfied to reach only those who came to church, Dad sought to reach out to people in the streets. In the early years in St. Paul, he would sometimes hold street-corner meetings, enlisting the help of young people in the church who could play a musical instrument or sing or perhaps speak briefly. He sometimes held weeklong nightly meetings in the church, never calling them revival meetings. The purpose was to call people to Christian commitment. One week's constantly repeated theme was "No Alibis, No Lullabies, No By-and-bys." As he developed this theme, he asked people to "be done with spiritual procrastination, to have no soft soap while ignoring society's wrongs, and to not defer to the hereafter the things we ought to be facing now—no alibis, no lullabies, no by-and-bys."[14]

Though he reached many through preaching, it was Dad's skill as a counsellor, one on one, which always fascinated me. This is a large part of a pastor's work, especially when people recognize that here is someone who accepts them as they are. A vast amount of a minister's time, effort, and private study and prayer is invested in helping people mend their broken marriages, assisting and encouraging them when they are down on their luck, helping them deal with illness, anxiety, or trouble with the law.

A man named John is long since gone, but I think he would not mind if the little kid he once knew recalled his battle with alcohol. Not to put too fine a point on it, John at age fifty was a wino, one of the street people of the 1930s who stumbled along Wacouta Street past the church, clothes rumpled after being slept in, chin stubbled from several days without a shave. He came in the church office one afternoon to see if he could have fifty cents "to get my shirts out of the Chinese laundry." Dad knew John wanted money for a drink, but he asked Phil Zuniga, a young Mexican lay preacher who was helping out in the office that day, if he would mind going with John to rescue his laundry. Dad handed Phil fifty cents.

"Oh, that's all right, Reverend," said John, "He doesn't need to come. I can get 'em myself." But Dad told him Phil had better go too, "to see that he got there all right," and the two of them left. They returned a few minutes later as John shamefacedly admitted to Dad that the laundry did not exist. Having surmised that from the start, Dad and Phil talked gently with him and helped him find a place at one of the nearby rooming houses. It was not a very fancy room, but sleeping there was better than waking up cold and stiff on a park bench. I don't know all that was said that day, but John became a Christian and was able to stay sober and keep a job. The next Sunday, John was in church, shaved and in clean clothes. Mother and Dad invited him home for dinner after church, and he told us stories of his life as a traveling salesman before he became an alcoholic. We would see him around the church frequently after that, visit him at his rooming house once in a while—a pleasant elderly man, who kept in touch with us even after our family moved away from St. Paul. He never took a drink again, rarely if ever would take any financial help, and got a job as a night watchman.

Dad always tried to address the need the person brought as well as his unrecognized spiritual need. One day he was scheduled to preach at the Minnesota State Penitentiary, an hour's drive from the church, and was hurrying to his car when a drunk man grabbed his arm and said he needed help. The obvious choices were to respond with "Sorry, I'm late for my meeting already" or "See my secretary; she'll set up an appointment" or possibly to call ahead to the prison, saying that an emergency had arisen and he would not be able to come. Dad saw no need for any of these. He said to the man, "I'm awfully sorry that I can't talk here, but why don't you ride along with me; we can talk on the way, and while I'm inside, you can take a nap in the car. And then when I come out, we can continue our talk on the way back." And that's what they did.[15]

Gradually, as the months went by, the people of First Baptist were reassured by their new pastor's quiet, attentive manner, his friendliness and concern, and his competence at his job. More important, they discovered that he liked them! It was not in him to be mean or retaliatory. He felt that there was something good in everyone. His working principle was "Accept what you can; don't be shattered by what you can't." He did not gloss over differences, but he genuinely believed that given time anyone could sit down with another and quietly and in prayer resolve any major difficulties. Hostility anywhere could be overcome.

As people recognized the integrity of Dad's belief and action, he became more and more involved in the church and city and across the state, in committees and in planning conventions and other meetings. He was invited to arbitrate the settlement of a strike at the Eagle Laundry in 1938. He accepted people whether they accepted his philosophy or not. In it all, the members of First Baptist Church saw him affirming the way of Jesus in his own life and helping to bring it into theirs.

And with this, the church became a community again.

As a small boy at the time, I was unaware of much of this process, of course. Church services mostly were rather long periods in which my main feeling was restlessness. But the church, under Dad's leadership, saw to it there were things for children, too. There was junior church, to which we kids marched out before the sermon. Once a month, the focus of junior church was "temperance day," which might feature objects pickled in a jar of alcohol or a blackboard analysis showing the difference in Saturday-afternoon expenditures of an alcoholic and a "real father." (The bottom line was that the latter's kid had some candy left over Sunday morning from his picnic in the park, while the alcoholic's kid had only a black eye to show for the weekend. Yes, it was a biased account, but not too far from the reality I have since seen as a physician.)

There were also church picnics. The Sunday school superintendent would tear off tickets, one per kid, which entitled us to an ice-cream cone at the park concession stand. Or we would all get aboard the stern-wheeler riverboat *Capitol* for a ride down the Mississippi. The steam calliope on the upper deck played as we cruised back home in the evening, the cars on the riverbank's highway slowing to keep pace with the boat and listen to the music. (For those of you too young to remember a calliope—accent on the first syllable—it's like a pipe organ powered by steam from the ship's boilers, and the sound really carries a long distance. A big one can compete with any number of amps a rock band cares to produce.)

There were church fun nights, too, for the whole family. New Year's Eve started at 8 P.M. with a two-hour talent show, featuring minstrels, drama, and music. The next hour brought food, followed at 11 P.M. by the watch night, a church service with singing. Then, at five minutes till midnight, everyone kneeled in prayer as the church chimes counted the minutes remaining in the year. Summertime did not bring nights like that, but it had vacation school, where fifty or a hundred kids would mill around making things out of wood, competing in memorizing Bible verses, or roaring out the school cheer under Dad's or some teacher's encouragement.

First Baptist Church was in the public eye again—but in a more favorable light. Membership was growing; the church's youth group was increasing; the spiritual outreach was on firmer ground. It was only natural that pulpit committees from churches in other cities began to cast a speculative eye on the man whose perception of God had helped bring this about. In 1938, after seven years in St. Paul, Dad received a call from the First Baptist Church of Syracuse, New York. He had a feeling that his work in St. Paul could now be carried on by the church congregation, under new leadership. In the previous year or two, he had been offered pastorates at First Baptist of Oakland, California, and at First Baptist in Seattle, as well as the presidency of Shurtleff College in Illinois. But the Syracuse church was a new and interesting challenge.

Dad announced his resignation in a letter dated 1 January 1939: "I have had other opportunities in recent years to go to churches twice as big, and with much more income, but believe that this [call] is from God."[16] The new church asked him to start March 1 at a starting salary of $6,000 per year, less $900 per year rent on the parsonage, with six weeks annual vacation. The rest of the family stayed in St. Paul to finish the school year, and in July, we moved to Syracuse, all except Margaret, who stayed on in Minnesota to finish college and to take a teaching job.

# Chapter 5

# Syracuse

*A two-thousand-member church presents a different set of problems from a small congregation, however much the individual members' needs are alike. To this was added the dilemma of reconciling Jesus' gospel of peace with a world bent on war.*

The First Baptist Church of Syracuse, New York, was decidedly different from the Minnesota pastorate Dad had left. There were few, if any, conservative farmers in this congregation. The business professionals, college students, and blue-collar workers who constituted First Baptist's two-thousand-member congregation were used to professionalism in their clergy. Dr. Luther Wesley Smith had just left the church for an administrative post in the denomination; before him, Dr. Bernard Clausen had distinguished the pulpit with his eloquent preaching.

The church was unique in owning and operating the Mizpah Hotel and Restaurant within the church building. One could enter a massive church auditorium through one set of doors or the hotel lobby through another. Church offices occupied the third floor; Sunday school rooms, the fourth; and hotel rooms, the fifth and sixth floors. The roof had a penthouse, where the full-time minister of music and his family lived (the church had six large choirs), and also provided access to the church steeple and fourteen-bell carillon.

This church was not divided by theology so much as by finance. The chairman of the trustees, a banker, felt that any assets accumulated should go to reduce the church debt, which stood at around $150,000, or should go into a savings account so that the church would be ready for any more lean years of the depression, which had devastated the nation in the past decade. Others foresaw an industrial boom as America prepared for war and envisioned growth in the city's industries. They wanted to improve the church facilities, anticipating an influx of new people.

In this instance, Dad sided with the progressives. He did not make a constant issue of finance, but at least once each year, he would preach on stewardship, the Christian's financial responsibility to support God's work, both in the church and across the world. Before his eleven years in Syracuse were up, the church was able to burn its mortgage.

In spite of such differences, the welcome was warm. People helped us move into the church parsonage on Ostrom Avenue in the university district. We were invited to barbecues, swimming parties, and church social functions. One man taught us boys how to drive a speedboat; another took us target shooting. No one was warily watching where the pastor's family sat; in this church it made no difference.

Both Mother and Dad seemed to fit right in. If Mother had any qualms about being first lady in a major city church, she didn't show it. She was gracious to all, but she adopted the business and professional women's group as her own project. This Sunday school class was mostly single women working as secretaries and clerks and some as teachers; many of them had no family in town and felt lonely in the bustle of the city. Mother not only taught them on Sunday, but at least once a month she invited them all to our house for a home-cooked meal. They idolized her, and some formed friendships with her that lasted long beyond our time in Syracuse.

## World War II

War appeared inevitable in 1939. Hitler had already seized Czechoslovakia and was stalking Poland when we arrived in Syracuse; we could hear on Saturday-afternoon radio his ranting speeches, with the buzz-saw antiphony of cheering crowds. Dad nevertheless remained convinced that war is morally wrong. Though his sermons consistently reflected this, he took personal interest in each of the young men and women of his congregation who joined the armed forces. He took them to lunch when they came home on leave, wrote them letters, counselled them in their times of need. When one young pilot was killed on a training flight, Dad grieved with the family, and in his study he kept, for the duration of the war, a broken piece of magnesium engine cowling from the plane. Gold stars were added to the church's service flag in memory of those who gave their life for the nation (there were about ten gold ones by the war's end, along with some two hundred ordinary blue stars representing all those in the armed services). There was never an attempt to instill guilt, never a criticism of their choice, only the warm personal support of a pastor for his people.

The congregation included several who chose the route of conscientious objector (C.O.) to war. Some of these joined the medical corps; others felt even that was implicit support of war that conscience could not allow, and they were confined to a civilian service work camp down near Elmira, New York. At least another three young people were Japanese American and had a particularly difficult time even though they were loyal American citizens. One of them was eventually "relocated" to one of the West Coast detention camps for Nisei. But each one, whether military personnel, C.O., or detainee, was the object of personal concern for my father.

Dad expressed his philosophy about war and peace in a radio broadcast entitled "The Minister and War" on Monday evening, 6 May 1940, over station WSYR. He reminisced briefly about his own decision not to bear arms or kill in World War I and then continued:

> Now it is 1940; once more the ministers of the church must seriously consider their responsibility to Christ. Nothing could be more important than that we study what the Master of men had to say about war and peace. Peace convictions must be founded in something deeper than party platforms. Unless they are rooted in the will of God and some basic religious philosophy, they will not stand up against the pressure of public opinion in wartime.
>
> What, then, is the religious basis for peace? I realize that there may be other approaches to the problem. There is the economic approach, with guarantees of world markets and national resources to all nations. There must be a plan of collective security with regional or world federations comparable to our federal union. There must be an educational approach, too, with intelligent propaganda analysis and exchange of cultural possessions. But as ministers of Christ we are primarily responsible for a religious contribution to peace, and the development of a universal conscience in relation to the world's chief collective sin. To that end, I would direct your attention tonight to the sources of our faith, as found in the Old and New Testaments. For as many of us learned to our cost in the last war, unless we have a Biblical and philosophical foundation for our convictions, we cannot stand before governors and before kings as spokesmen of the Holy Spirit.
>
> Increasingly, those of us in Christian ministry feel that something must have been seriously wrong with the interpretation of the Gospel, during these two thousand years of its history, to have resulted in such a flood of hatred and destruction as is now let loose on the earth. The world cannot continue to organize for lying and treachery and death, and at the same time preserve its soul.[1]

This radio speech prompted objections and cautions from Dad's own church congregation, who had not quite bargained for this type of pronouncement from their new pastor. W. Brewster Hall, one of the church leaders, wrote a friendly letter of caution to "go easy on anti-preparedness. People in church are criticizing."[2] Levi Chapman, an elderly businessman who generally approved of what was currently happening at First Baptist, nevertheless reasoned that "preparedness doesn't mean a nation will fall; nations that fell did so because they had not prepared enough."[3] Despite these objections, the church board reaffirmed its policy of free speech in the pulpit. One anonymous radio listener, however, sent the offer of a free one-way ticket to Russia.

Dad welcomed the church board's opinions, praising them for speaking out—too often dissenters in church remained silent (at least to the pastor's face). "But," he continued, "people come to church asking what has the gospel of Christ to say?" He agreed that governments must be prepared for war. His concern was the degree and the possibility of universal military training becoming permanent law. With the wrong people in power, the government can then become "totalitarian to save democracy from becoming totalitarian."[4] He invited Hall, Chapman, and other laymen to his home for a discussion of the dilemma.

People apparently wanted to hear such preaching even though they might personally disagree. The new preacher made them think, and he never expressed disapproval of someone else's honest opinion. In fact, he seemed to go out of his way to present all sides of a question and then offer what was, for him, the answer closest to the mind of Jesus. Church attendance grew.

## Church Worship

There was a certain amount of formality and dignity to Sunday morning worship in this big church, to which Dad adapted but which he also modified with his conversational preaching style. It was a team effort, really. George Oplinger, research chemist and dean of the Syracuse Society of Organists, could evoke majestic thunder or quiet folk melody from the massive pipe organ that dominated the choir loft above the platform and pulpit. As the more tardy of the worshipers seated themselves in the semicircular rows of pews, George would conclude the organ prelude and begin the opening bars of the processional. The a cappella choir— the first string, so to speak—could be seen unobtrusively getting in step rhythmically to the music as they waited in the foyer. As choir members entered through the doors at the rear, each began singing, marching across the rear aisle, the two halves meeting at the center, then down the main aisle to divide again as they ascended the steps on either side. John Clough, the minister of music, impeccably dressed, smiling, walking at a measured pace, brought up the rear. The scene was even more impressive on Palm Sunday, the week before Easter, when all six choirs marched, each person carrying a palm branch in celebration of Christ's triumphant entry into Jerusalem.

The need of the moment could always overrule formality, however, and Dad developed an ability to stay calm and in charge of the situation in any circumstance. He need only utter the prearranged signal, "There is a platform emergency," to bring several alert ushers to the aid of anyone in distress, someone who had fainted, perhaps, or who was having an epileptic seizure. He even taught the church ushers a "code of conduct," emphasizing the need for being prepared for the unexpected and for doing one's job as inconspicuously, yet cordially, as possible. Sometimes he handled the problem himself. One Mother's Day, his sermon was interrupted by a distraught middle-aged woman who came down the aisle in front of the pulpit. Dad paused in his preaching, knelt down on one knee at the edge of the platform to speak quietly with her for a minute or two, and then returned to the pulpit to continue his sermon after explaining to the congregation that this was one of our fellow members who had had troubling news about her son and who sought our prayers.[5]

## Other Controversies

Dad spoke and acted on controversial subjects ten or twenty years before more conservative leaders reached consensus. One was race. Some of the staff of the Mizpah Hotel, not necessarily church members themselves, would follow the custom of that era by quietly making it very difficult for an African American to get a hotel room. This brought them into conflict with the pastor and other church people, who would occasionally make reservations for visiting church leaders only to have the guest discover, when he showed up at the hotel desk and the clerk saw him for the first time, that there was no reservation. Dad would then intervene.

"But, Mr. Dahlberg," the flustered manager would protest, "we can't do that. It will ruin our business. You wouldn't want a Negro in your home, would you?"

"Why, of course I would," Dad would respond, "and they are in my home often. But it suits this gentleman's convenience to be downtown tonight. I do remember making a reservation for him, and I would like you to find it." And the manager, bowing to the inevitable, would thereafter treat the guest as any other. But with a new clerk, it sometimes began again.

Prayer in the schools became a national issue in the late 1980s, but Dad was addressing it forty years earlier. He opposed prayer and Bible reading sponsored by public schools and based his argument on three points:

When my own grandfather was starting my father, Elof, in school in Fergus Falls, Minnesota, the one thing he wanted to make sure of was that there would not be prayers in the school sessions. My grandfather was right in his position that prayer and Bible reading are the responsibilities of the parents in the home, not of government and political officialdom.

Those who are advocating legalized prayer as a part of our educational system need to realize what a Pandora's box of problems and human ills would escape from that box if public prayer and Bible reading in the schools were adopted. Our situation today is very different from the situation at the beginning of our country. Today we not only have Protestants, Catholics, and Jews, but Hindus, Buddhists, Muslims, and all kinds of various cults. Whose sacred books are we to read? The Koran? The Hindu scriptures? Or the life and teachings of Buddha?

In Syracuse in the 1940s an effort was made to develop a program of prayer and Bible reading that would satisfy everybody. A Jewish rabbi, a Protestant minister, and a Catholic priest all agreed on what Bible passages were suitable for reading in the schools and the whole program of procedure. It didn't work; many teachers were unprepared to say a prayer in public, and were unfamiliar with the Bible. The captive audience became bored and restless, and it all became a matter of dull routine.[6]

The state churches of Europe have daily periods of worship in the schools, some of them lasting for an hour. Yet there is a smaller attendance by far in the churches there than the attendance here in the United States. The trouble is that the parents in the state churches think that the religious faith of the youth of the nation has been taken care of by the schools.

Some might object that in many homes there is not so much as even a table blessing at meals, let alone family worship in the home. That is unfortunately true in too many instances. In the early church, however, people's faith was strong and Christianity spread by word of mouth without government backing of any kind. When Emperor Constantine realized how rapidly Christianity was growing, he made it the official state religion of the Roman Empire, thus increasing his own political power. Whole tribes and nations became "Christian" rather than people individually experiencing Jesus as Savior and

Lord, and religion was no longer one's personal responsibility, but that of the state. If we want to see Christianity at its best today, we will find it in our foreign mission fields, even though that is where the new Christian often experiences complete rejection by friends and family. It is there that Christians feel impelled from within to go out and tell others of their new-found faith.[7]

Dad also wanted church-sponsored schools to get their funds from entirely outside the government. He believed that government subsidy, no matter how well intentioned, would inevitably be followed by government supervision.

## Pastoral Ministry

Dad's life was not just one policy pronouncement after another, however; actually, they were few and far apart. A minister's main job is to look after the spiritual life of the church, both as a group and as individual people. A large church of two thousand members cannot be managed by one person, any more than an army regiment can be run by only one officer. Syracuse First Baptist had a full-time staff that included the minister, an assistant minister, a director of Christian education, two directors of music, two office workers, and two janitors, not counting the hotel and restaurant employees. Besides meeting together on Sunday morning and evening and on Wednesday night, the congregation had youth groups, Sunday school classes, choirs (with private voice lessons), women's groups, men's groups, Boy Scouts, drama groups, and a center for visiting servicemen and servicewomen, as only a partial list. A building is meant for use.

Dad always got along well with his church staff, particularly with the succession of young assistant ministers and the ministers of music, John and Gertrude Clough. The only potential staff member I ever remember him rejecting was a candidate for stenographer whom an employment agency sent over. "She kept clicking her false teeth the whole time she was taking dictation," said Dad. "She would have driven me crazy if I'd had to listen to that all the time!"

Two assistant ministers recall some of his advice and humor.

John Schroeder: "Years later, when we sent out the announcement of our third child's arrival, we mentioned that though her name, Linnea, was Swedish, we could not claim any drop of Swedish blood. Your Dad sent us a note of congratulation which included a sizeable red dot. Your father explained that he was donating a drop of Swedish blood to help make her name legitimate."[8]

Woody Clark: "I learned there that a 'home-going pastor makes a church-going people' with the result that I have put a heavy emphasis upon pastoral visitation all through my ministry. I recall the time he [Dahlberg] introduced Louise and me as prospective members of the staff. He said, 'I took one look at Louise and decided that any fellow who could win a girl like that would make a good assistant pastor.'" Woody always made sure that Louise was with him whenever he candidated for any church after that. Her insights and questions were always part of the decision to accept a church's call. In Woody's words, "A pastor's wife should never try to be the pastor of the church, but the church has to live with her in the parsonage."[9]

During one sermon, Dad whimsically let the congregation in on what occasionally passes through a minister's mind during that long choir processional at the beginning of church. "A minister is not always as solemn as his face might indicate," said Dad. "His mind can wander, just like anyone else's. I might be wondering what would happen if I should suddenly wink at the altos, then casually stick out my foot and trip John Clough as he marches by. And for those of you who have asked how George Oplinger at the organ always knows when to start playing softly just two sentences before I finish the morning prayer, the fact of the matter is that George is the one who decides when I have prayed long enough and lets me know it's time to stop, in this musical way."[10]

The pastor believed that Sunday school should be not only instructive but also enjoyable. It was not a babysitting service, except for those under one or two years old. Ernest Bowden, a newspaper writer for the *Syracuse Post-Standard,* once toured First Baptist and reported, "We all meet people who hate church because they were compelled to attend in childhood. But children who attend here ask eagerly, 'When will it be Sunday again?'"[11]

A conservative estimate of that portion of a two-thousand-member congregation who at any one time are ill or in some major crisis and who request pastoral help is 10 percent. In addition, the pastor tries to visit each member or family occasionally even when they are not in trouble. There are weddings and funerals and classes for those who wish to become Christians. There are committees—deacons, trustees, Sunday school teachers, building maintenance, and many others. There are committees and groups outside the church that require the minister's time. A minister without executive abilities is in trouble. The job also requires compassion, scholarship, and street smarts. Congeniality and a spouse committed to the work, besides, are very good indeed.

Dad's pastoral specialty was marriage counselling. It had been the topic of his first book, *Youth in the Homes of Tomorrow*.[12] Not only did he spend a significant amount of time in trying to help people mend their broken marriages, but he would not perform a marriage unless the couple were first willing to discuss certain basic concepts of marriage. He wrote:

> Seventy-two per cent of Protestant pastors have no premarital conference, and 85 percent have no systematic follow-up. There are several important points to cover: I explain to couples the differences between masculine and feminine psychology by which husbands and wives can learn to understand each other's minds. I instruct them in money management, since marriage is a business partnership as well as a romantic union. Earn it honestly, spend it intelligently, save it diligently, distribute it generously and justly. I interpret right and wrong attitudes towards sex from Christ's point of view, and refer the couple to proper clinics for instruction in planned parenthood and intelligent spacing of children. I try to teach them to be emotionally controlled, morally sound, and religiously active in their faith.[13]

A pastor's wife will usually be personally involved in church life in addition to managing a home and family. Mother once was asked how she coped with all her activities. She replied with the story of the farmer who each day added yet another egg to the collection under a setting hen, giving as his reason, "Just want to see how far the old fool can spread herself."

Mother had a natural talent for the role of minister's wife. She served on the council of the YWCA (Young Women's Christian Association) in Syracuse and at one time or other had taught Sunday school classes from kindergarten age to adults. She could always find an extra plate for the unannounced guest at mealtime. She wrote down phone messages with accuracy. Notification, during one of her women's class dinners, that a snake had escaped from Bruce's collection upstairs and was now wound around the rung of a chair occasioned a crisp order for me to go to the neighbor's house two blocks away and get my brother back home fast. This was one of the few times that she was near panic, Bruce recalls. Snakes were no longer welcome in the house thereafter, caged or free.

Mother would tolerate no bad language from her children but was more lenient toward those for whom it was habitual. A wartime sailor on a railroad station platform once asked her, "Ma'am, could you please tell me where in hell the station waiting room is?"

She explained in a neutral tone, "Well, it's really not in hell at all. It's down those stairs and through the corridor to the left."

There were times in Dad's life when he needed to be alone—not just when Mother would shoo us out of his study so he could get his sermon done on Saturday morning, but time away to meditate and pray. Opportunities were rare, but he made it a point, once a year, to spend all night alone in prayer out under the sky. He continued this practice for more than thirty years until increasing age made it difficult. During those years, his time of prayer might have been spent in a rowboat in the middle of a lake or on a ship at sea; he might have been miles out in the desert or high in the Rocky Mountains. Once, when he was at a conference in Scotland, he spent a night of prayer on a cliff overlooking the cave where the first missionary to Scotland took shelter centuries ago. He never talked about these times much, except maybe in a diary or a family letter. Most other times, he was available whenever the phone rang or someone met him on the street.

Dad consciously worked at being easy to talk to, besides having a natural talent for it. No matter how long the line at the church door, he was there till the last person went out. If a small child had something to say, he would squat down to be on the same level. He would listen smilingly and patiently to elderly, deaf Mr. Rubyore recatalogue, in his quavering voice, all the places he had been during his eighty-odd years, "Rome? Yup, I've been there! Shanghai, too! Winnipeg? Been there many times!" (At Mr. Rubyore's funeral some years later, Dad wryly remarked, "At last, we're talking about a place where our good friend has never been before!")[14]

If someone's problem would take a while to discuss, out would come Dad's date book, to be thumbed through briskly as Dad would say, "Now let me see. How would Tuesday at 10:30 be? We could take time to talk this through then."

If Dad was at a loss for someone's name (which rarely happened), he would continue to shake the person's hand while saying, "Now, your name again is . . ."

"Smith," the man would prompt.

"Yes, of course, Mr. Smith, but I was trying to recall your first name . . ."

"Oh . . . George," the man would reply, pleased that he had been recognized. (It worked equally well if the visitor's initial response was his first name.)

Dad could not possibly make all the needed house calls himself and often enlisted the aid of his staff. Occasionally this caused mild trouble.

Fred Allen, one of the assistant pastors, wrote to him when Dad was away, "Clough and I called on Mrs. B. last Monday. She greeted us at the door with 'Well, is the world coming to an end?' I asked her why she made such an inquiry and she replied that you had been there Sunday, and now we appeared. She said that since Clausen's day [about twenty years earlier], no minister had called. During our conversation it came out that Schroeder, Clark, and Al had all called over the years. I told her, 'Mrs. B., you are the most called-on member I've met!' She replied, 'Them's assistants. You don't count them!' Clough told me, 'Now, Fred, you know how you rate!'"[15]

Dad's manner with young people was relaxed and easy. Speaking to the young people of the church one Sunday on the topic of original sin, he observed that young people often asked him just what it was all about. "Let me assure you," he said, "that original sin has nothing specifically to do with anything about sex." This piece of good news caught my young attention immediately. I was a little vague on the subject myself, but guessed it had something to do with our being blamed for whatever it was that Adam and Eve had been up to in the garden of Eden. So if it was not about that, what was it? It was not that Eve ate the forbidden fruit, he continued, nor that she persuaded Adam to try it, but that she put her own way ahead of God's will. Dad went on to explain that the refusal to depend on God, the insistence on doing things our own way (which we can almost always justify to our own satisfaction) is at the root of sin. We often disobey in this manner, but God is understanding and forgiving when we acknowledge it and when we ask help in overcoming it.

Dad often said that if you want to stay young, travel with young people. If you want to get old, try and keep up with them! He was a popular speaker at youth meetings and could often be found at some ice-cream counter with a group of them after the meeting. And in the strong and growing youth group in his own church, influenced not only by him but by the teachers and leaders he had helped assemble, at least six young people went into the foreign mission field, and six more into the ministry.

During these years, Dad took an increasing role in the affairs of the Northern Baptist Convention nationwide, in addition to his local responsibilities. He was a frequent speaker at conventions and at the national assembly grounds in Green Lake, Wisconsin. By 1946, he and Mother had become active in a number of committees and programs beyond the local church. At that time he was a member of the American Committee of the World Council of Churches (WCC), the Marriage and Home

Commission of the Federal Council of Churches, the board of managers of the Northern Baptist Publication Society, the board of managers of the New York State Baptist Convention, the board of trustees of Colgate Rochester Divinity School, the board of directors of The Ministers Life and Casualty Union, and the local Rotary Club; an early member of the Fellowship of Reconciliation and the American Baptist Peace Fellowship; and vice president of the Commission on Evangelism for the Federal Council of Churches.

Mother, in 1946, was chairwoman of the Women's American Baptist Foreign Mission Society's Candidate Committee and president of the Ministers' Wives Association of the Northern Baptist Convention.

That year, yet more responsibility was to come.

# Chapter 6

# National Leader

*Edwin Dahlberg's ability to reconcile conflicting parties did not go unnoticed among Northern Baptists. This was an era when differing views of Christian responsibility were threatening to tear the church apart.*

Dad once heard Jawaharlal Nehru, India's prime minister, give a speech in which he warned, "You start out with a vision of what you want to do. As time goes on, some constituents are dissatisfied, and you are tempted to adjust your attitude. As the adjustments go on, you end up having kept your constituency but having lost your vision."[1] Dad now would face a similar dilemma. Except for 1845, when American Baptists split into the Northern and Southern Baptist Conventions over the issues of slavery and of fair representation, there has probably been no greater storm among Baptists than the conflict between the liberal and fundamentalist factions in 1946 and 1947.

Strengths sometimes can have a downside. Baptists take a strong stand for freedom of conscience, freedom of worship, and complete freedom from government control. They also claim the ability and responsibility of each person to interpret the Bible according to the leading of God in that person's own heart. These principles were behind the Virginia Baptists' insistence in the 1780s on specific guarantees in the U.S. Constitution, resulting in the Bill of Rights.[2] Unfortunately, these same principles were also behind the firm conviction of many individual Baptists that only their own beliefs and conclusions are correct and that everyone who has reached other conclusions is, therefore, mistaken at best or deliberately subversive at worst.

To understand the depth of division between religious fundamentalists and liberals (both of whom are firm in their loyalty to the teachings of Christ), we might consider their respective viewpoints on two issues. The first issue is the use of the Bible to evaluate opinion, belief, and behavior. "Is it consistent with the Bible?" is a question both sides frequently ask because the Bible, written over a period spanning more than a thousand years, is a written standard available to anyone.

Conservatives, particularly fundamentalists, guard their interpretation of the Bible jealously, believing that every word was put there by God in just the order one sees it (in the original language, that is, but there are plenty of scholars able to translate from the original Hebrew and Greek). Thus, if the Bible says that Jonah was swallowed by a big fish and got out alive three days later, then that is exactly what happened. There is no room for figures of speech or for allegory, no admission of inconsistency. "If you start to doubt even one passage, how can you believe any of it?" is a question that typifies this doctrine, which is known as "the inerrancy of Scripture."

Liberals, on the other hand, believe that God inspired humans to write the Bible but was not standing over their shoulder dictating word for word. The message is from God, but some study and understanding of the times in which the respective human authors lived give a more accurate sense of what is being said. The liberal is more likely to ask whether an interpretation of a certain passage, taken in context, is consistent with the message of Christ and the prophets as a whole.

The second issue is the central purpose of collective Christianity, otherwise known as the church. The conservative emphasizes bringing individual humans into a relationship with God through Jesus: "Believe in the Lord Jesus Christ, and thou shalt be saved."[3] Correcting the wrongs of the world is God's province, though God may use humans to bring this about. The liberal emphasizes a need to deal with social injustices, such as starvation, war, poverty, and oppression, as a means of making individual humans aware of the love of God, helping those who have been estranged to open their hearts to the Holy Spirit: "Thy Kingdom come. Thy will be done in earth, as it is in heaven."[4] Thoughtful people in the middle, and some leaders of stature in each camp, understand the necessity for both approaches. As we have seen, Dad's mentor, Walter Rauschenbusch, claimed that without both personal evangelism *and* social action, we do not have the gospel.

## The 1946 Convention

At the annual convention of Northern Baptists, which met in Grand Rapids, Michigan, in May 1946, matters grew steadily more tense between the liberal and fundamentalist factions, leaving a large majority in the middle wishing that the church could get on with its mission. The point was reached at which the opposing sides were hissing each other's speakers. A delegate recalls one encounter in the men's washroom in which one of the liberal leaders happened to come face-to-face at the washstand with a fundamentalist opponent. The latter, enraged at the jaunty satisfaction of the other, who had just won a vote on the convention floor, pointed a finger and sputtered, "I'll get you, one of these times!"[5] However, the account of the convention, below, is offered not as a collection of anecdotes but rather as a description of one man's way of dealing with controversy.

As a local newspaper reported, "Unanimity struck sessions of the Northern Baptist Convention only once, Thursday, as debate raged most of the day to plague Mrs. Anna Swain, Convention president."[6] A Pennsylvania delegate began by moving an amendment that the contribution to the Federal Council of Churches (FCC, a favorite target of conservatives) be stricken from the budget.[7] It was only a $14,000 item in a $4 million budget, but debate surged back and forth, tangled for an hour in *Robert's Rules of Order,* before the amendment was voted down. Other debates arose about centralized funding, about sending out missionaries who allegedly did not believe the gospel, and about who should lead the convention in the obviously difficult year ahead. The only thing everyone agreed upon was that President Harry Truman should not have an official personal representative to the pope in the Vatican.

The business session on the morning of Thursday, May 23, was given over to an attempt to reach agreement on policy to which officers and missionaries of the Northern Baptists must adhere. The joint purpose of the several thousand churches represented at this meeting was to support missionaries and administrators who would spread the message of Christ worldwide, but the representatives wanted to be sure these appointees understood Christ's message as they themselves did before giving them financial and moral support.

F. W. Fickett, of Arizona, presented a motion which, in essence, directed

> That the Northern Baptist Convention . . . not employ as secretaries or appoint as missionaries any persons who refuse to affirm the following:
> (a) That the record of the Incarnation of our Lord Jesus Christ . . . is true and trustworthy.
> (b) That the Resurrection of Christ as stated [in the Gospels] is true and trustworthy.

(c) That the record of the miracles of Jesus as given in the Gospels is true and trustworthy.

(d) That the New Testament is inspired of God in all its contents and that the acceptance of its historical facts, revelation, teachings, and doctrines is obligatory in Christian faith and practice.

Many delegates realized that this resolution would open up endless debate on the exact interpretation of many passages of the Bible and, moreover, would subject missionaries to a detailed creedal test. They saw this as contrary to the basic Baptist belief that every Christian is competent to interpret the Bible under the guidance of God, without dictation from other humans.

Rev. Winfield Edson, of California, presented a substitute motion: *"Be it resolved:* that we reaffirm our faith in the New Testament as a divinely inspired record and therefore a trustworthy, authoritative and all-sufficient rule of our faith and practice. We rededicate ourselves to Jesus Christ as Lord and Savior and call our entire denomination to the common task of sharing the whole Gospel with the whole world."

The substitute was adopted in place of the original resolution.[8] It passed almost unanimously because most delegates considered it a noncontroversial statement of their basic faith. As it turned out, different interpretations of this affirmation during the following year would lead to yet more conflict.

During preconvention committee meetings, when Dad was attending a meeting of the board of managers of the Publication Society (the educational and publishing arm of the Northern Baptists) and Mother was attending the candidate committee of the Women's Foreign Mission Society, Mother heard a rumor in the mission society meetings that Dad was being considered for president of the convention. This was apparently the first that he had heard of it, but when the nominating committee reported to the business session of the convention several days later, it proposed Dr. Edwin T. Dahlberg as president. The fundamentalists proposed an alternative slate of officers led by Rev. L. J. Julianel of San Francisco. At the vote in the Friday, May 24, session Dahlberg was elected with about twenty-five hundred votes out of a possible four thousand.

The new president of the Northern Baptist Convention (NBC) customarily was invited to give the closing address of the meetings and then take over the duties from the retiring president. Dad struck a conciliatory note, which most delegates welcomed; he deplored "the cold, abstract liberalism and its diluted gospel, and the dry literalism that fails to release out of the Bible its joy, gladness, and liberating power as a living book."[9] Both camps—the liberals and the fundamentalists—as well as those on middle ground, felt there was hope for keeping the Northern Baptists together. The magazine *Missions* in its June 1946 issue proclaimed, "Not the liberals nor the fundamentalists, but the denomination has spoken."[10]

## Tenure as NBC President

Acting upon the one unanimous resolution of the Grand Rapids convention, Dad joined nine other Protestant leaders in a visit to President Harry Truman to urge him not to retain an official U.S. representative at the Vatican. President Truman, himself a (Southern) Baptist, was really irritated at this request. "You people are upsetting the apple cart!" he told the delegation (meaning, probably, "don't complicate matters I've already worked out").

"It's not us," countered the delegation leader, Methodist Bishop Bromley Oxnam. "Your decision breaks the division between church and state." In the end, Truman held firm in his plan. Episcopal layman Myron Taylor, who had spent much effort trying to avert World War II and to get other countries to accept Jewish refugees fleeing from the Nazis, continued to be U.S. envoy to the Vatican.[11]

Other than that, the first few months of the Dahlberg presidency of the Northern Baptists went fairly smoothly, although he did have to correct an Associated Press misquotation of a comment he had made. In a report titled "When Do We Start?" Dad, as president of the convention, was quoted as saying that every doctor should spend some days in a hospital bed and every preacher a year in the penitentiary. Dad pointed out that what he had said was "a year in the pew," not "a year in the pen."[12]

Many of the fundamentalist leaders approved of Dad as president of the NBC, seeing him as a bridge between the fundamentalist and liberal camps. Dr. Murk of the conservative Temple Baptist Church in St. Paul wrote Dad in a letter, "Frankly, if we have to have a liberal in the office, I'd prefer to have you to any other liberal I know."[13] W. B. Riley, the grand old man of fundamentalism in Minnesota, congratulated Dad on preaching a sermon on evangelism to which he himself subscribed most heartily.[14]

Some of the liberal leaders grew overconfident. Rev. W. Abernethy of New Hampshire wrote to Dad, "I hope Beall, Pierce, Bradbury, and the rest will now understand that the denomination is not inclined to go the

way they have been trying to take it. Such a defeat they suffered at Grand
Rapids!"[15] Dr. C. Oscar Johnson of St. Louis, looking ahead to the next
annual meeting, predicted, "The Fundamentalists are not strong enough
numerically, even if they had the right spirit, to take over the affairs of the
Convention."[16] While this was true, it did not take into account another
possibility—that of secession.

The problem, as the fundamentalists appeared to see it, was that the so-
called all-inclusive policy allowed missionaries to be sent out who did not
personally believe in some doctrines the fundamentalists considered
essential: for example, the virgin birth of Jesus (that is, the doctrine that
Jesus' mother, Mary, was a virgin when Jesus was conceived; therefore,
Jesus was the Son of God in a biological as well as a spiritual sense) and
the infallibility of each passage of the Scriptures. They thought it had
been settled by the resolution at Grand Rapids. Since all had agreed on
the divine inspiration of the Bible, the fundamentalists thought the church
should live up to the policy it had made.

The liberals, and many in between, thought it had all been settled by
the overwhelming vote that missionaries should not be tested by any set
creed. Acknowledgment that the Bible is inspired by God and acceptance
of Jesus as Lord and Savior defined a Christian. The liberals, too, thought
the matter had been settled by the resolution at Grand Rapids.

Neither side could yield, as a matter of principle. The fundamentalists,
while still in the NBC, formed their own Conservative Baptist Foreign
Mission Society and were talking as well about a separate Conservative
Home Mission Society (mission work ministering to needs within the
United States). In the midst of this was E. T. Dahlberg, raised among conservatives and educated among liberals, who hoped to heal the widening
breach. He wrote his friend N. T. Mears, now the Baptist state president
in Minnesota, asking for a meeting between the two groups there. Mears
was in favor of it, but the Minnesota board would only agree to a meeting between Dad himself and the executive committee of their own
board.[17] The vote on this and other related matters was consistently thirty-
six to six, with Mears in the minority.

Compounding the controversy, the NBC's financial office in New York
operated under the so-called unified budget principle, coordinating competing requests for church money. They received funds from churches
nationwide and distributed them to the various missions, state boards, and
other collective enterprises. The office now refused to release mission
funds, even funds contributed by conservative Minnesota churches, to the

group who objected to the NBC selection of missionaries. Meetings were held, personalities clashed, tempers flared, and the purpose of the church was forgotten; yet each side believed itself to be championing the will of God.

There was a period in early 1947 when it looked like the breach might be healed. Both sides wished it to be so. Dr. Earl V. Pierce, a conservative and former NBC president, said that if the convention had been willing to "add a few words to close the gap through which a very few undesirable missionaries occasionally slipped," they could have saved the day.[18] Dr. Charles Seasholes and Dr. Hillyer Stratton, both in the liberal group, denied that the inclusive policy was in any way contradictory to the existing evangelical policy. Each missionary, each Christian, was still free to interpret the Scriptures and could not be held accountable to one way of interpretation held by a minority—or by a majority either, for that matter.

From there, all hopes of unity began to unravel. Each side interpreted the ambiguous (perhaps intentionally ambiguous) wording of the previous year's policy statement to support its opposing, nonnegotiable stance.

Jockeying for position at the upcoming 1947 annual convention, some conservatives attacked Dad's politics by publishing a report of the Congressional Committee on Un-American Affairs that listed him as one of the petitioners for presidential clemency for communist Earl Browder. Dad issued a general letter:[19]

> This statement is true. The implication that I have had some relation with the Communist party, however, is not true. . . . I did write in petition for the release of Browder from prison. This I did as an American and a Baptist, believing that according to the Bill of Rights no man should be put in prison in this country for his political or religious beliefs, even though guilty of fraudulent passport statements as Browder undoubtedly was. In this stand I believe I am in the best tradition of Roger Williams, the founder of our Baptist fellowship in America. Subsequently, though not because of any influence of mine, presidential clemency was exercised, and Browder's sentence commuted from four years to fourteen months, which would seem to be sufficient penalty for any passport irregularity.
>
> For most of our lifetime, we have been suffering from an evangelism of division. This kind of evangelism has divided Baptists in half a dozen ways. We are now Roger Williams Baptists, Conservative Fellowship Baptists, Convention Baptists, Regular Baptists, Middle of the Road Baptists, and

Southern Baptists in the North. How much longer is this fragmentation to go on? Do we not need now an evangelism of reconciliation? . . .

Let us be much in prayer for each other. Not just that other groups may be won over to our particular pattern, but that all of us together may be lifted up to the high levels of God in Christ, where we shall see everything from a new point of view. . . . As Count Keyserling once said, "Problems are never solved. They are dismissed, in the presence of a higher unity."[20]

Dr. Harold Porterfield of Madison, Wisconsin, chided Dad about the Browder statement: "I know you are not a Communist, and believe you acted sincerely in that Browder position. But when you are a minister, and especially when president of a large religious organization, you are foreclosed from individual political action. Churches cannot work together for the Kingdom of God as long as they, the churches, are taking active part in political controversies. Let us, I say, keep to our business of making people Christian, and they will then take care of political and economic questions *as* Christians."[21] Dad thanked Porterfield for the fine Christian spirit in which he wrote but went on,

It was necessary for me to make the statement that I did because of the widespread charges that had been circulated in many of our Baptist State Conventions concerning my political affiliations. The petition that I signed back in 1940 was, of course, long before the present questions had become so acute, and before I was an officer of the NBC. I do not think, however, that I can quite agree with you that a minister or convention officer should not engage, individually and personally, in political action. He is still an American citizen, and therefore has an obligation to his country. . . . If the Christians in Germany had mixed a little politics with their religion and not have left their church life in a vacuum, the Nazis would never have come into power.[22]

Amid all the politicking, other work of the Northern Baptist Churches continued. As the 1947 annual meeting approached, Dad and the NBC had accomplished much. A series of youth convocations across the cities of America had involved hundreds of teenagers and young adults in "The Discipleship Plan," a personal commitment of high-school and college-age students to Christian service. Accompanying a team of several college-age young people, Dad personally took part in three or four of the thirty-six convocations, each of which lasted a day and a half and was usually preceded and followed by a long train journey. One of his teammates, Roger Fredrikson, recalled years later how Dad stayed up most of one night on the train, from Cincinnati to St. Louis, talking about Christ with a traveling magazine salesman.

Another accomplishment was the World Mission Crusade, which in raising capital funds for worldwide mission work exceeded its $14 million goal by more than $2 million. Plans were in progress for an evangelism crusade for the coming year. Northern Baptists participated in agricultural relief projects for Europe. Farmers sent a planeload of hatching eggs to Poland with the message, "When the shells burst which this plane carries, they will burst with life, not destruction."[23]

In addition, Dad traveled tens of thousands of miles speaking and listening to Northern Baptist churches around the nation, gaining a grassroots understanding of what each church felt about the cooperative work of the denomination.

These various successes should have brought great encouragement to the Northern Baptists meeting in Atlantic City, New Jersey, and eventually they did. But in May 1947, all accomplishments were overshadowed by other events. On May 10, just days before the convention opened, Dr. W. B. Riley of Minnesota wrote a polite letter of personal resignation from the Northern Baptist Convention. He felt that the fundamentalists no longer had any voice there. He wrote, "The Foreign Mission Society refused to make the virgin birth a condition of commissioning [new missionaries]—a Unitarian triumph." He also protested NBC funds for Minnesota going to a "minority group" and not to the fundamentalists.[24]

At a preconvention caucus, fundamentalists formalized their withdrawal from the Northern Baptists to form the Conservative Baptist Association (CBA), resulting in a split-off of approximately one thousand of the seven thousand churches of the NBC. Many more young pastors privately wondered if there was any future for them in this denomination that could not seem to get its sense of purpose together.[25] Roger Fredrikson recalled his feelings on that day when, as a twenty-three-year-old student, he was left wondering, "The fiery guys [eloquent preachers] are gone. We lost something here. Who are we? What am I going to do?"[26] Several others who were there have recalled a similar feeling of bewilderment.

Morale was at a low ebb as Edwin T. Dahlberg stepped to the microphone to give the opening keynote address at Atlantic City. In contrast to the tension among the delegates, his manner was calm and relaxed. He began to speak about the time when Moses and the children of Israel were in the wilderness and had lost all faith in God or themselves; they were wandering blindly around and around the mountain known as Mount Seir. Their situation had to change if they were to reach the land promised them in Canaan. He quoted Moses as saying, "Then the Lord said to me, You have compassed this mountain long enough; turn northward!" (Deuteronomy 2:2-3). He continued:

> We have our own denominational Mount Seir, a mountain of theological and organizational controversy which has dominated every horizon of our Convention since the close of the First World War. From year to year, the controversy has changed emphases—one year evolution, one year the New World Movement, then the authority of the scriptures, or the resurrection and the second coming. Now it is the virgin birth, the inclusive policy, proportional representation, and the Federal Council of Churches. Controversy has become an obsession with us, and we go around and around it. Whatever the issues, we have become increasingly divided into many separate fellowships. Is it not time we were having some fellowship in the Christ who died for all? Let's make an end of controversy with ourselves and begin one with the world . . . over the 9 billion dollar liquor traffic, the gambling syndicates' growing strangle-hold on our nation's politics and recreation, the divorce rate of one out of every three marriages, the systematic efforts to involve our nation's youth in the same militaristic philosophies that have sent two whole continents into a hell of death and anguish, the lack of active involvement of our nation's people in a church—in some states as low as 27%. On this one thing we must be firm: We need more cooperation with other Protestant bodies, not less. The technique of Communism is said to be to locate the points of tension in the world and aggravate them; the task of Christianity is just the opposite, to locate and seek to relieve them.[27]

This "Turn Northward!" address, as it came to be known, seemed to mark a turning point. People who were there cannot define the magic, but many of them—conservative, evangelical young pastors at the time with a less extreme outlook than that of some of the fundamentalists—agree that it was Dahlberg who crystallized their resolve to stay in the NBC and work together.

Business sessions were yet to come. That same afternoon a California delegate reintroduced a version of the creedal statement of the year before, more specific in detail, and requiring "employees of all [NBC] agencies, boards, and committees to accept without question these plain, self-evident, uninterpreted New Testament statements [essentially the statements presented in the previous year's resolution] concerning our Lord as at least one condition of employment or appointment by the Convention." This was to be voted on the following morning. At that time, school principal W. E. Saunders of New Jersey offered a substitute motion: "That, believing that the Grand Rapids resolution [of the previous year] clearly expressed the will of our people, this Convention again refuses to make *any* creedal statement a test of fellowship and service." The substitute motion was adopted by a standing vote.

Immediately, E. M. Poteat of New York presented a resolution for later consideration: "Whereas, The Conservative Baptist Association of America has publicly announced its organization, which has an adopted creed and constitution and elected officers, and which will function in complete separation from, and independence of, the Northern Baptist Convention, be it: *Resolved,* that the Northern Baptist Convention . . . publicly and with regret . . . states that the Northern Baptist Convention and the Conservative Baptist Association of America are separate and distinct organizations." This was scheduled for a vote at a business session two days later.[28]

On Thursday, when the motion was brought back to be voted on, Dad rose to preside during the afternoon business session. He later confessed that he felt totally inadequate to handle the situation. Sensing the hostility on both sides, "everyone . . . sitting on the edge of their seats, wondering is this guy for or against our side? I prayed silently, 'Lord, help me!'" At such times, Dad's usually open and friendly facial expression would take on a look of grave attentiveness. He paused at the microphone a moment, decided that this was a point at which the presiding officer should offer some unsolicited advice: "I believe it would be a great courtesy to the Convention if the gentleman who made that motion would withdraw it."

There was a brief consultation on the convention floor; then Poteat rose again. "Mr. Chairman, I have consulted with my second, and we would be happy to withdraw it."[29]

Impressed with his diplomacy and faced with a continuing need to navigate uncertain waters, the members of the nominating committee approached Dad to ask him to consider an almost unprecedented second term. He was dubious and said he would have to consult with his family and his home church. When he broached the subject to her, Mother burst into tears: "Oh, Teddy, not another year of this!" But she agreed, if the children and the church would agree. Dad phoned us children, explaining to us that it would mean his being away from home a lot for yet another year. Margaret was already married and had two children. Bruce and I were in college in Syracuse (he was on the GI Bill, and I was finishing my freshman year). All of us were agreeable and felt it was kind of an honor for him, as did his assistant at Syracuse, Fred Allen, and the church leaders he consulted. But Dad said it was Bruce's words that most helped him make the decision: "Dad, if they want you, there must be a reason. I'd say take it!"

So began another year of extensive traveling and committees. The Baptist magazine *Crusader,* in a summary of what the president of the NBC does, reported that Dad traveled a total of 74,000 miles in the United States and 11,000 more in Europe.[30] He accomplished this while continuing to direct the work at Syracuse First Baptist Church, which by then had 2,300 members, 141 of them new that year. Under his leadership the congregation raised $85,000 for the World Mission Crusade. A vast amount of correspondence also crossed Dad's desk each week. Among other duties at the time, Dad was president of the Syracuse Ministerial Association and was on a commission to investigate the feasibility of merger between the Northern Baptists and the denomination known as the Disciples of Christ. "I was optimistic about this until I learned that the commission had been studying the possible merger for eighty years," he remarked to me later. He was also one of the NBC delegates to the Baptist World Congress in Copenhagen in 1947, after which he visited Baptist relief work in thirteen European countries.

He continued to work for reconciliation between the NBC and the new Conservative Baptist Association, but there was little communication between the two groups. As an article in the magazine *Missions* put it, quoting George Bernard Shaw, "The one lesson of history is that nobody ever learns the lesson of history." The Conservative Baptist Association, formed on a provisional basis at Atlantic City the year before, met prior to the Milwaukee convention in 1948. Five hundred delegates now set up its constitution, "calling on all Bible-believing Baptists to associate for fellowship without any interference in their local church autonomy."[31] By its wording, this invitation could have been issued equally well by the NBC itself, but the CBA was making a political statement in hopes of attracting more churches to itself.

During the last week of his two-year term as convention president, Dad was concerned about the advent of universal military training (UMT), or peacetime draft. This was a presidential election year, and there was strong debate on the subject nationwide. The 1948 Northern Baptist Convention at Milwaukee passed several resolutions concerning U.S. policy. They opposed complacency concerning war and moods of hysteria and hatred and rejected the idea that war is inevitable. A study group on militarism quoted the *Army and Navy Bulletin* of 18 January 1947, which had claimed, "Today the Army has virtual control of foreign affairs. . . . the chain of control in diplomatic hot spots both in the execution of basic policy and in the formulation of *ad hoc* arrangements lies almost totally in the hands of military authorities." The resolution noted that "A successful military career is not in itself alone assurance of full and adequate qualification for public office; therefore, be it *resolved* that we protest to the President and Congress of the United States the growing tendency to use military men in civilian posts, and call for the immediate restoration of civilian control of policy-making power."[32]

The convention's program on Saturday evening featured a town-meeting discussion of UMT. Participation was brisk and prolonged, finally ending at 9:30 P.M. Bernard Clausen, prominent Cleveland pastor, and Walter White, secretary of the National Association for the Advancement of Colored People (NAACP), spoke against UMT. They recommended reduction of world tensions by welcoming displaced persons into the United States and by increasing relief to stricken countries of Europe and elsewhere. They also urged lessening the "infiltration of professional military minds into the policy-making departments of American government." Dr. Daniel Poling, pastor and member of President Truman's study commission on UMT, and Perry Brown, chairman of the American Legion Security Commission, argued that strength through (military) preparedness decreased the chance of war and predicted that the United Nations would eventually have a police force to maintain law and order. Poling cited democratic Sweden as an example of a peaceable nation in which UMT in some form had existed for 136 years.[33] This debate continued among Baptists for several years, during which time UMT became a fact of national life.

## World Council of Churches

As immediate past president of the NBC, Dad was asked to be one of the convention's representatives at the newly forming World Council of Churches (WCC) at its initial meeting in Amsterdam in the summer of 1948. The World Council was a loose association of 147 church bodies in over forty-four nations (the number of church groups has grown to over 250 now), which gathers every five years to discuss matters of mutual interest. A ninety-member Central Committee, of which he was also a member, directs the work of the WCC between meetings and meets yearly to hear reports on the state of the churches in other countries, to seek consensus on matters of theology, religious education, interchurch cooperation, and evangelism, and to oversee the work of the WCC's disaster relief organization, Church World Service. It is not a so-called superchurch and has no authority over its member churches. The purpose of the initial meeting was, not to solve the problems of the world, but to bring about a renewal and awareness of worldwide fellowship of Christians.

Not all member churches were represented in Amsterdam. The Hungarian Lutheran bishop named to the Central Committee had been placed under house arrest by the (Communist) Hungarian government. No response was heard from the Orthodox Church of the Soviet Union, but six Iron Curtain countries had allowed delegates to attend. The Roman Catholic Church declined on constitutional grounds, and several other groups refused in principle to cooperate with those who did not hold their own beliefs.

During the week of meetings, Dad attended several services of Communion, among them one sponsored by the Lutheran Churches of the world. He reflected that he was probably the first member of his family in a century to do so and wondered whether his four grandparents were turning in their graves. But as the congregation approached the altar rail in groups of twenty, he secretly hoped that it would be the bishop of Sweden who served him, and it turned out to be so. As the bishop offered the bread and the cup, he said, "The blood of Christ, shed for thee," and Dad felt that a great chasm had been spanned. As he recalled years later, "I didn't become a Lutheran, nor did the bishop become a Baptist, but both of us were brothers in the Kingdom of God."[34]

Dad spent six years, from 1948 to 1954, on the Central Committee of the WCC. Two sessions are particularly notable. After the 1950 meeting in Toronto, he helped write a three-page report in *Missions* magazine on opposing apartheid (then being proposed as official policy in South Africa), on peace in the shadow of the Korean War, on displaced persons (World War II refugees, many of whom were still homeless and stateless after five years), and on ecumenical (cooperative) evangelism.[35] Some of the WCC statements of 1950 brought repercussions the following year that the committee members had not fully foreseen.

East-West tension characterized the 1951 meeting of the WCC Central Committee at Rolle, Switzerland. The publication of the pronouncements from Toronto on the Korean War and on nonrecognition of China had stated only the majority (Western) viewpoint, putting Eastern churches' continuing existence in danger and their leaders' lives at risk. Bishop Chao of China, one of the seven co-presidents of the World Council, did not attend but sent a letter of resignation, saying that the Committee majority's public pronouncements had put him in an impossible situation with the Chinese government. He affirmed his freedom and his loyalty to Christ but chose to stay in China to minister to the Christians there.

Bishop Bereczky, of the Hungarian Reformed Church, said he would have done the same in Chao's situation. He pointed out that the Eastern countries were in the midst of a massive repudiation of imperialism and colonialism with which the Christian church was associated in their minds. The language of the pronouncements from Toronto, he said, made no recognition of what Hungarian and other churches had said against it, putting him in a difficult position with his own government as well. "It would have been more polite," Bereczky continued, "to leave my name off the report since I had so little time to become acquainted with it. Three requests: One, leave my name off the report. Two, [and off] the Ecumenical Study Commission. And three, that my name be omitted from the Central Committee and I be considered only as an observer."[36]

Dad recounted in his diary that there was rather timid applause to this statement, noting the courage of the respected old man who made it as well as the serious difficulties it portended for a worldwide Christian fellowship in a world torn by war and strife. The bishop was urged by the Committee to dissociate himself only from the report and not from the Committee.

In a private letter to us children, Dad wrote that two of their sessions had been closed to reporters and he was not allowed to speak about them for fear of endangering the lives of Christians behind the Iron Curtain.[37] He did mention, however, that the Chinese Communists had executed his friend Dr. Henry Lin, who had been a guest speaker at the 1947 Northern Baptist Convention. Lin had once headed the printing of Chinese paper currency, supervising several paper mills as well. However, he gave it up to become president of Shanghai University, saying he "would rather make men than money." Dad noted in his diary in 1951:

> There is little difference between the churches of occupied countries of Norway and Holland during the war and churches in occupied countries today. If we are sympathetic to the pastoral approach, we must remember that American Christians are looked upon with great suspicion in China, and great responsibility rests upon the Christians of India, therefore, to keep up personal contact with Christians of China. Wherever there are trade missions, or

political missions, let WCC scrutinize the personnel to see if there are Christians on the commission with whom there may be personal and private conferences.

Our report on conscientious objection aroused one of the most vigorous debates of the week, which went on for nearly three hours. In presenting the report, I made clear that we were not debating the merits or demerits of conscientious objection [to war] but were simply defining the position of the C.O. before the law, in the light of universal declarations on religious liberty. Dr. Boegner [of France] submitted an amendment urging the duties of C.O.s as well as their rights, a proposal we gladly accepted. However, some of the other proposed amendments would have emasculated the report. The most vitriolic attack on it was by Archbishop Athenagoras of the Greek Church, where two C.O.s are now under the death penalty and many others in prison. Many others spoke against the report, to the extent that Kenneth Grubb of England handed me a note suggesting that we had better withdraw the whole document. I told him we could not consent to do this, and when a couple of the World Council secretaries and presiding officers also suggested it, for once I became stubborn and said we wanted a showdown.

The debate then began to swing the other way, with Martin Niemöller of Germany, Bishop Berggrav of Norway, and Ernest Brown of England, all speaking on behalf of the report. The vote finally, at 7:15 P.M., was about ten to one in our favor, which really surprised me. I was very happy about it, because I believe it represents a step ahead in religious freedom and world peace.[38]

Some have charged that Dad was an impractical visionary who had no experience with war and that, therefore, his ideas on the subject were of little value. The question has been asked, "Would he still be a conscientious objector if he had been confronted with Hitler?" Yes, he would—I have argued that question with him more than once—and though he believed that Hitler might have been nipped in the bud before war was necessary and that a different handling of postwar Germany in the 1920s would have kept the problem from arising to begin with, he still firmly, stubbornly, believed in peace and in trust in God rather than armed force.

Note that the three men Dad mentions in his diary who supported his view in the WCC debate did in fact have extensive experience with war. Martin Niemöller, a German U-boat captain in the First World War who became a pastor, was imprisoned by Hitler from 1938 till he was liberated by the Allies in 1945. Bishop Berggrav was one of the Norwegian leaders who maintained the defiant spirit of the Norwegians in the face of the Nazi armies. Ernest Brown, a member of Winston Churchill's cabinet, helped write British legislation on conscientious objectors. War was fresh in the memories of these men.

In July 1950, Niemöller wrote in a memo, "In past, various nations have been willing to let themselves be convinced of the necessity of war, and to look on it as a lesser evil. . . . People must not be left in doubt that Christians, and therefore the church, can no longer be rallied to violent solutions. The churches' voice cannot be silent anymore. . . . The impression that the Christian Church believes that a war can, in any way whatever, be justified by those who start it must become absolutely impossible."[39]

What Dahlberg and Niemöller and leaders like them were doing, and would continue to do despite vilification, was keep alive a vision of a world of peace and justice under God. Dad would have further ample opportunities in the years to come.

## Simultaneously, a Pastor

Dad's work was not all world meetings, of course. He was still pastor of First Baptist Church in Syracuse, and most of his day-to-day work was concerned with helping his 2,300 church members with their spiritual problems, conducting weddings and funerals, preaching, administering the many groups within the church, serving in community organizations, answering letters, planning ahead. A minister's average day is spent half in the office, half in the community's hospitals, jails, and homes. Most evenings, there are meetings to go to: deacons board for the spiritual church program, trustees for the management of the church's physical assets, Christian education for the Sunday school and children's programs, Wednesday-night church supper and prayer meeting, and Sunday-evening church service. Though the pastor may not actually be a member of the Boy Scout troop, the junior-high, senior-high, and young-adult groups, the girls' guild, the women's missionary society, the men's group, the choir, the membership committee, and a dozen others, it is politic for the pastor to look in on their meetings and show an interest.

The help of an able staff kept things at Syracuse First Baptist going well in the late 1940s. At the same time, many other churches who were seeking a new pastor included Dad on their list of potential candidates. Given the combination of circumstances, Dad was open to new challenges.

One that caught his attention was a church in suburban St. Louis—Delmar Street Baptist Church. I had just been accepted at Syracuse Medical School and was congratulating myself on not having the expense of going away from home to school. I now discovered that home was going away from me, as Mother and Dad prepared to move to Missouri in the fall of 1950.

# Chapter 7

# St. Louis

*Although Northern and Southern Baptists had divided at the time of the Civil War, there are a few mid-America churches, such as Delmar of St. Louis, that carry dual membership. In his new pastorate, Edwin T. Dahlberg could be active in the affairs of both the North and South.*

Delmar Street Baptist Church was on the downtown edge of suburban St. Louis. The membership was cosmopolitan, with Washington University college students from many countries, teachers and business executives of both northern and southern backgrounds, and people from the local neighborhood. Although many of the younger people had (for the 1950s) a progressive attitude on racial issues, a number still had been brought up and taught in the South. Delmar Church held membership in both the American (Northern) and the Southern Baptist Conventions and contributed generously to the mission and educational programs of both groups.[1]

Still active in world religious affairs, Dad was a member of the executive committee of the Baptist World Alliance and an American Baptist representative on the Central Committee of the World Council of Churches. But when he began his pastorate at Delmar, just as at Syracuse, he was a pastor first. Committees, writing, and traveling took lesser priority, and only with the approval of his congregation.

Dad liked his new church, as he had his previous churches. He told with delight of one of his first Sundays there, teaching an adult group of about one hundred when he was commandeered by two five-year-old members of the beginners class. They had been sent by their teacher to see if he was free to come to their room and inspect a model of a home in Nazareth the little children had made. The two had searched all over the church for Dad, and when they found him, they blissfully disregarded the hundred adults to whom he was speaking. He remembers, "They opened the door, all starry-eyed, and said to the astonished company,

'Hello!' Complete silence for a moment, and then they said, 'We want Mr. Dahlberg.' So I went out with them, and they told me with great glee that I was to come in with them to the Primary Department. I was properly overcome with wonder and amazement, and we all had a great time. The mothers, and the primary superintendent, were about ready to fall through the floor when they heard about it, but I don't know when I have enjoyed anything more."[2]

New church members received special attention. Dad explained just what he wanted them to do, so that no one would be caught unawares or be embarrassed. In one letter to new members, he wrote,

> At the close of the sermon next Sunday I am going to ask the new members to come forward to the very front pew while we sing the invitation hymn, and I am going to say just a few words of welcome to them at that time. Then I shall go from one to the other to speak to each one personally and to give each one the "hand of fellowship." This is one way of showing how happy the church is to have you as new members. After the hymn has been sung, I will ask the new members to rise and stand together.
>
> If it is possible for you to come into the study at about 10:30 A.M., before the morning worship service, I would like to have a word with all the new members at that time.

Two of the new members on that Sunday, husband and wife, became leaders of the congregation in the years following, and the letter was still among their mementos in old age.[3]

## Racism and Housing

Dad entered into the civic affairs of St. Louis, an act consistent with his belief that if you do not have both evangelistic outreach and Christian social action, you do not have the gospel of Jesus Christ. In a family letter, he told us,

> I am attending the National Housing Policy Conference which is being held here. Today's sessions were intensely interesting—especially the addresses by Raymond Foley of Washington and Mayor Lawrence of Pittsburgh. Tomorrow morning we are going on a tour of slum areas and new housing projects here in St. Louis—a three-hour trip which ought to give a good idea of the conditions in our new home town. We wind up for a lunch at the Anheuser-Busch Brewery at noon, as their guests. My conscience hurts me a little about this, but for the sake of seeing the housing conditions I'll take a chance. The breweries and taverns are such a force for the pulling down of the home that it seems contradictory, but I'd like to see what kind of a liaison there is.[4]

He saw quite a bit—people living in the midst of rats, rubbish, outdoor privies, and horse manure. He found himself in alliance with Monsignor O'Grady, head of the National Council of Catholic Charities, as he and the monsignor supported some of the black delegates in a vain effort to get some reference to Negro housing problems in the findings of the conference. "Some of the Alabama real estate men said we just didn't understand, and that we were leading the conference down a blind alley." He was struck with the contrast between the housing conditions and the efficiency of the brewery that hosted the lunch—"Millions of bottles moving in steady rows through the filling, bottling, capping, and labeling machines, and room in the basement for 110 freight cars at the loading platforms." He did not intend the contrast to be interpreted favorably.[5]

Race relations was a problem more difficult (or perhaps just more obvious) in St. Louis than it had been in Dad's previous pastorates. He was both optimistic and cautious on the racial outlook of the city. One day in 1951, he spent a couple hours at an all-day brotherhood program at one of the high schools and had observed that in dramatic sketches and square dancing, whites and blacks of both sexes had paired off in a most natural and democratic fashion. He felt satisfaction in having baptized the man who headed the program. Dad noted that the only speech during his visit had been five minutes by Henry Fonda, who was in town for a stage presentation of *Mr. Roberts*. Fonda had visibly impressed many of the students by saying that people had to be educated into intolerance, just as they did into algebra.[6]

Dad was more wary in responding to my query about bringing a black medical-school classmate home for Thanksgiving holiday:

> By all means bring him along. But there are some difficulties you should be aware of in advance. It will be very difficult to find a movie or a restaurant which we could attend together. He probably runs into these things in Syracuse, but here it is much tougher, where even the schools are still segregated. I don't think there would be any difficulty at church. There might be some raised eyebrows among the older adults—about 70% were raised in the white supremacy tradition in the South, but they are pretty broad-minded in the main. The young people would not even give it a second thought. I'd very much like to have him come—it would mean more than a dozen sermons on race relations.[7]

In any event, my friend declined the invitation, citing a previous commitment.

Dad was appalled at the injustice done to a Louisville journalist, Carl Braden, who in 1954 had sold his home to a black with the result that someone had dynamited it. Carl, rather than the dynamiter, was sentenced to twenty years in prison under the Kentucky sedition law for "inciting to riot which might lead to the overthrow of the government." He was released after eight months when the Supreme Court ruled state sedition laws unconstitutional. His wife was also jailed, only for eight days, but their children, ages one and three, had been left in the house alone after the arrests until neighbors came in the next day. Five years after this event Dad opposed the efforts of a senator from Mississippi who was trying to reinstate the sedition laws.[8]

The 1951 conference on housing evidently had done little to improve the slums of St. Louis. In 1955, Dad called attention to slum conditions again:

> Last week we read in the papers about a little two months old Negro baby, Reginald Harrington, who was terribly bitten by a huge rat while asleep in his crib. I went down to the hospital to see that baby. All the finger tips of his right hand had been bitten. His forehead had been bitten—one place the size of a quarter gnawed away. The whole upper rim of his right ear had been chewed off. The flesh on the back of his left hand and arm had been nibbled away as though someone had peeled an orange. As I looked at this little boy, I was filled with a kind of holy anger—anger at the tenement owners, anger at the garbage inspectors, anger at the people who consistently block better housing, anger at ourselves as citizens and church members who permit such public inertia.
>
> Make no mistake about it. God stands in the midst of us with his plumb line. Not in bad housing areas alone . . . but in every institution of society. We cannot live forever in a house that is out of line with the will of Almighty God.[9]

Public attitude changes slowly. Dad nudged it where he could. That same year, he invited a Southern Baptist friend of his to speak to the church youth group at a three-day study session. Clarence Jordan was known (some southerners might have used the word *notorious*) throughout much of the South for his farm near Americus, Georgia, a cooperative effort by several families, both black and white, working in equal partnership. Jordan had had bomb threats, had been shot at while driving his tractor, and was socially ostracized, but he persisted in his belief in racial equality, and his farm survived. In fact, it has done quite well over the years. Teenagers and college students were entranced. Jordan's conference at Delmar in early 1956 had a small but significant fallout later that year when Delmar Church opened up its gym floor to interracial basketball, under the leadership of the youth pastor, Dick Broholm. In congratulating the Delmar senior-high team for a 56 to 53 victory over the Kinloch Baptist Church, Dad told them a YMCA secretary said Delmar's entrance into interracial basketball set the pace for the entire city.[10]

## Labor Relations

In 1955, Dad was already foreseeing the future problems of unemployment. This was before the days of multinational corporations' moving jobs overseas but was in the midst of the great drive for automation that began to change American factories after World War II.

In one of his sermons, he observed that already General Motors had a single machine that could work on 104 V-8 engine blocks simultaneously; that Corning Glass had fourteen machines, each attended by one man only, that turned out 90 percent of all the electric light bulbs in the United States, and that Raytheon was producing one thousand radios per day with only two workers to do what two hundred workers did before. Dad noted that thousands of jobs were bound to disappear over the next few years, even though production would increase and standards of living would eventually go up. In that sermon, Dad reflected on the work situation:

> It will require the most thorough cooperation of labor unions and management, plus a high degree of Christian social conscience on the part of the whole nation. We will need to make much larger provision for education. Still more, we are going to need a greater concern for our relationship to God. What is going to be the effect of a shorter work week, and more leisure, on character? Are we going to turn more heavily to gambling, materialism, divorce, and crime, or are we going to turn to the God of Jesus Christ for a new and dynamic spiritual life?
>
> A company official in the Ford Motor Plant in Cleveland, proudly pointing to a new automatically controlled machine, said to labor union president Walter Reuther, "You can't collect union dues from those guys." To which Reuther replied, "Neither can you get them to buy Fords." And let me add still further, Neither can you get them to worship God. It is when machines do our work that we are going to be most in need of God, lest men decay.[11]

## Student Counselling

The same easy conversational manner and active curiosity that enabled Dad to talk with physicists, pilots, or factory workers also made two-way communication possible with college students. One of his most publicized addresses was to the student body of McKendree College in St. Louis, in which he gave an account of his choosing the ministry and advised the students how to make the best of their own options. Quoting Methodist bishop Richard Raines, he told them, "Ask yourself, where is the world's need greatest? Where is the struggle hottest? Where are the laborers fewest? Where is the battle fiercest? Answer these yourself . . . then ask, Do I have any talents that make me available for that kind of service? For where the need of the world and your talents meet, that is where you are called of God to go!"[12]

He often addressed the needs of those going away to college or into the armed forces: "Don't be ashamed of your religion. You do not need to be a pharisee about it. Be humble, quiet, and modest. But be true, for there are those who love you and there are those who care."[13]

Presented with questions about which he had little knowledge, Dad was often able to give relevant counsel despite his admitted lack of immediate information. Answering a student's query about the Zoroastrian religion, he replied,

> I don't know too much about Zoroastrianism, except that it has an ethical emphasis of a rather high order. It's no easy job to persuade a non-Christian of the need for Christ. . . . In general, I think the main difference is not one of ethics but of the power of the risen Christ. No other religion represents God as seeking His people in the same sense that we find Him doing so in Christ, as defined in John 3:16. As one Chinese said, "My own religion taught me what is right, but Christ gave me the power to achieve what is right."[14]

Dad restated his conviction about the distinctiveness of Christianity in a 1957 sermon:

> It is this basic faith that God is like Jesus [thus he turned the simile backward from the usual and made it more understandable] that will finally win. If we are prepared to wager our very lives on the spirit that Jesus exemplified in his relations with both God and humanity, we cannot lose. Even death itself must yield to it. . . . Christian victory is never satisfied with overcoming the world by winning of wars. *It must win the enemy, and abolish the enmity.* Such was the victory of Christ on the cross.[15]

## Emilie as Pastor's Wife

As Dad's own career developed, it was strengthened by his marriage. Mother was not one to view her own lack of a college education as an obstacle. She did indeed maintain a warm home and was a fine mother to us three children, from our infancy through adulthood, but she had talents in her own right. I have already mentioned her adoption of the women of the church who had no families of their own (see chapter 5). She also championed the wives of students, saying that they had a double job to do, not only being wives, but being a help in the completion of their husbands' education—a triple job if there were also children. She also served on the national board of the Women's American Baptist Foreign Mission Society (WABFMS), an organization that oversaw the needs of the many single women missionaries overseas. (The WABFMS and the American Baptist Foreign Mission Society later merged into a single group known as the Board of International Ministries.)

"Standards are higher in all fields now," she said in a 1963 interview. "So much more is expected in Christian education. It now includes a world-wide interest, not just the country of one missionary of the church. We have classes to help women understand the womanhood of the world. The world is much smaller, and we want to know all about it."[16]

Equally important with her service in the church and on boards, Mother gave Dad intelligent companionship on many of his journeys, accompanying him to meetings in Europe and Asia and across the United States (mostly during the Delmar Church years, after we children were grown). She also served as a gentle critic, calling Dad to account at Sunday dinner for an occasional misstatement in his sermon. As my brother, Bruce, put it, whenever Dad soared too high into the realms of idealism, it was always Mother who brought him down to earth again.[17]

On one occasion after the Sunday sermon, Mother asked Dad, "Teddy, what was the point of that story you were trying to tell this morning? Was there something we missed that should have been funny? You looked so baffled when nobody laughed."

Dad looked troubled and repeated what he thought had been a pretty clever sermon illustration, "Well, Emilie, this newly married couple is trying to get some privacy, but the waiter keeps hovering over their table. The husband finally tells him they'd like some honeymoon salad. 'Honeymoon salad, sir? What's that?' asks the waiter. 'Lettuce alone!' says the husband."

Dad looked expectantly at Mother, who laughed and said, "That's the trouble, then. In the pulpit, you said, 'Lettuce only.'"

Dad was not averse to telling stories on himself. He was once at a breakfast with a group of black pastors in St. Louis and was hoping someone would pass the sugar and cream. These had been kept at the other end of the table since everyone else was apparently drinking their coffee black. He finally blurted out, "Would some of you black-coffee lovers down there please pass the cream?" There was dead silence as his companions misinterpreted what he had said, many construing it as a racial slur. There was no calling the words back or trying to explain them, and Dad's face reddened each time he recalled the incident in later years.

His sense of humor was rarely tickled more than when he traded stories with his crony C. Oscar Johnson, the jovial pastor of St. Louis's large Third Baptist Church. One of their favorites was of a farmer who came down from the back country and entered a men's clothing store in the city. He told the clerk he wanted to buy a set of underwear.

"And what style did you have in mind, Sir?" asked the clerk.

"Oh, hit don't make no difference," muttered the farmer.

"Any brand preference?"

"No, hit don't make no difference."

"Well, did you want a summer style, or long woolens?"

"Don't make no difference."

"How about the color?"

"Hit don't make no difference," the man explained. "Hit's for a corpse."

For several months afterward, whenever Dad and Johnson were sitting together on some committee and the discussion of some church matter grew dull and pointless, one would softly comment to the other, "Hit don't make no difference . . . hit's for a corpse."

Even when not joking, Dad had a lack of pomposity and a lack of self-consciousness which put others at ease. Whether sharing his faith in a street-corner conversation or having lunch with some of his staff at a neighborhood diner (where, after serious study of the menu, his choice was invariably a hamburger and hot-fudge sundae) or picking up paper someone else had left lying near a public trash can or responding to a vitriolic letter from a critic, he always responded to the need of the moment in a nonthreatening manner.[18]

Dad's presidency of the NCC put a strain on the church office staff. His secretary, Lois Brackman, reminisces:

> Dr. Dahlberg dictated all his letters. . . . The volume increased considerably, and one of our members purchased dictating and transcribing equipment so that he would be able to work anywhere. She even provided for extra help to do the typing. Dr. Dahlberg tried, but after two or three reels (it was before tape when wire was used for recording) he gave up, saying he just could not talk to

a machine. . . . The letters he prepared were very well done, clear and in good order, but apparently he tried so hard to make everything perfect that he wore himself out pushing buttons and making corrections. So—we stored the equipment and went back to personal dictation, which I appreciated as much as he did.

The correspondence did pile up a bit with his many trips out of town, but when he returned, he would start at the top with the letters most recently received so that at least some folks would have a prompt response. Then he would continue through the pile, apologizing for his tardiness. The most letters I ever took at one sitting was seventy-nine. His dictation was never hurried or boring, however. He took a personal interest in each correspondent, and as an interesting incident regarding the writer or the letter would come to his mind, he would stop and tell me about it. I always enjoyed those comments. I think that was what he missed in talking to the "machine." I know I did.

He never dictated sermons or speeches. Those he typed himself on an old manual typewriter. . . . everyone received a kind reply. He never turned away anyone who came to the office, whether he was dictating, studying, or whatever, unless he was in conference with someone else at the time. That was also the only reason he would not accept a phone call. He was always accessible to any caller; Dr. Dahlberg enjoyed every encounter.[19]

## Travel

In 1961 Dad was invited to preach to a group of fourteen churches at Oak Ridge, Tennessee, near the Atomic Energy Center. He wrote:

The most interesting part of the week were the visits to the atomic energy plant and the Institute of Nuclear Studies. I guess I spoke to more Ph.D.'s per square foot down there than any place I have ever been. There are fifty of them in the United Church where I spoke Sunday morning, seventy more at the Presbyterian Church, and about the same proportion in all the rest. The institute's director is a physicist who is also an ordained Episcopal minister—he has an amazing capacity for lecturing on scientific and religious subjects alike. I heard him give a two-hour lecture to forty Ph.D.'s on "The Origin of the Universe." On all these tours, I tried to look intelligent, and I learned that my guide later told someone that I actually had asked some intelligent questions, but it's like a different world.[20]

During their last full year at Delmar, in 1961, Dad and Mother used their vacation time to travel to India and Burma. In India, they attended the 125th anniversary celebration of the Assam Baptist churches. "The meetings were tremendous, with 8,000 marching through the streets of Gauhati, probably two-thirds of them young people," Dad wrote. "There were eighteen hill tribes in full regalia, spears, feathers, knives, and all. A new experience for me was the mass translation system, whereby a dozen interpreters stood in various sections of the meeting hall, all translating into separate languages simultaneously."

The two of them moved on to New Delhi, joining several friends for the third assembly of the World Council of Churches. It was a strenuous two weeks of "grinding away at reports, resolutions, and findings," and afterward they took a two-day holiday trip to Nepal with a St. Louis friend, Father Edward Duff, one of the Roman Catholic observers at the WCC meetings. Katmandu seems to have stuck in Dad's memory more firmly than the committees of New Delhi. He and Father Duff were taking pictures when both were suddenly butted from behind by a surly Brahma bull: "He seemed of a mind to toss both the Protestant and Catholic clergy clear over the Himalayas. Fortunately he had only broken, stubby horns, so no harm was done—except to our dignity, which some of our enthusiastic American friends further injured by shouting 'Olé!'"

After a visit with my own family in Burma,[21] Dad and Mother returned home by way of Hong Kong, where the Church World Service agency of the WCC was heavily into relief work for the millions of refugees coming out of Red China. They inspected noodle machines that made a high-protein supplement for refugees and visited Haven of Hope, a TB sanatorium. Once they were nearly mobbed in a free-for-all during distribution of clothing and blankets.

Arriving back home, Dad commented on the world church scene. The present state of Protestantism was not what Jesus had had in mind. He then told a modern-day parable: "One of America's most famous football coaches had a disastrous season some years ago. Calling all the squad together after a particularly humiliating defeat, he said, 'Boys, you played a magnificent game—each one in his own position. The trouble was in the spaces in between your positions. That is where our opponents came through.'"[22]

This has been the problem with the churches, Dad said. Each denomination of the Christian church today is playing a reasonably good game in its own position. The trouble is in the spaces between the positions. This is where the powers of evil come through—materialism, communism, militarism, gangsterism, racism, and false doctrines of every kind. Cooperation between the churches can fill these gaps.

Dad was referring in part to continuing racism in America. This was the period when the freedom riders were testing bus integration in interstate travel in the South, often receiving beatings for their efforts. He himself had attended an "illegal" meeting of white and black pastors in Birmingham, Alabama, in 1960, in defiance of a city ordinance prohibiting such meetings.

And already some voices of change were being heard. At the 1961 Southern Baptist Convention, a missionary returning from Nigeria chided the twenty thousand delegates, saying that Southern Baptists were eager to hear all about the African mission, providing that they did not have to entertain any of the products of the mission. It was very disillusioning, she said, to be invited to a church as a missionary speaker but to be cautioned that it would not be wise to bring one of the Nigerian Christians with her. She received a storm of applause, and people swarmed up on the platform to meet her after her speech.[23]

Shortly afterward, Dad attended the combined baccalaureate services of three black colleges in Atlanta, staying at the home of Dr. Benjamin Mays, the president of Morehouse College. He heard of several students who were to have received their diplomas but who instead were in jail for their freedom ride. Dr. Mays had told them never to seek martyrdom, but not to be afraid of it if it comes. When one young woman was asked why she had refused bail, she answered, "Because if I ever have a daughter, I don't want her to go through again what my generation has suffered."[24]

## Retirement, Sort Of

In November 1962, one month short of his seventieth birthday, Dad retired—from the full-time pastorate, at least. He looked with satisfaction at his final weeks as pastor of Delmar: sixteen new members by baptism, a dozen more by transfer, two of the young men of the church presenting themselves for the medical mission field, six of the younger business executives in the church mapping out support for the new pastor, the year's budget underwritten almost completely on the first day of the financial campaign, and the building in its best condition in years.

One of the finest events of the last week was an Alcoholics Anonymous (AA) meeting that Dad attended in order to see his "favorite alcoholic" receive a gold card for having been off alcohol a whole year. Dad recalled, "He was one of my worst alcoholics, too, in so many bloody fights and arrested so many times. He almost shook my faith during the five years Larry [Loughhead, the assistant pastor] and I have been working with him. He told me, 'I used to think I was no use to God or anybody, but then I began to think that if people as busy as you or

Mr. Loughhead could invest so much time and money and faith in me, I must be good for something.'"

Delmar Church gave Dad and Mother a retirement party. The speakers included a ten-year-old girl whom he had dedicated as a baby, a college student he had baptized eight years before, and a young couple he had married. The church presented a silver tray and an insurance annuity guaranteeing them $2,000 annually for the next ten years. "You will excuse the long letter," Dad wrote his children, "but a fellow doesn't retire every day. I have three addresses ahead this next week, but meanwhile Mother and I are leaving tomorrow on a three-day retirement honeymoon up at Macon, Missouri."[25]

The essential ingredient of enjoyable retirement is not the absence of work. It is rather the opportunity to continue some work, but control the schedule. Dad kept fairly busy for five months with committee tasks and speaking appointments, set months before, between his official retirement date and the time he and Mother actually left St. Louis in the spring of 1963.

He also continued to make hospital visits, often starting his day at 6:30 A.M. visiting someone before surgery and then staying with the patient's family while they awaited news from the operating room.

In that in-between time, they traveled west to Denver to visit his surviving sister, Effie, and my own family. (I was on a year's home leave from the mission hospital, continuing a surgical residency that had been interrupted five years before.) They then flew back to St. Louis for a final week of packing and farewells. The furniture was sent off on a Friday. Mother and Dad then stayed with their friends the McCarthys for two nights of rest before driving east. Dad's concept of rest, anyway.

On Friday night, he gave a sabbath address at the United Hebrew Temple. On Saturday, he made rounds on the church's shut-ins, one last time. When Dad stopped off in the psychiatric ward of a hospital to congratulate a man who was ready to be discharged home, the man asked him if he would visit a sixteen-year-old boy in a nearby room who had been crying out ever since he had been admitted to the ward earlier that day.

> As I was walking up the corridor to the young lad's room, I could make out just one word, repeated over and over again in the most agonizing tones, "SOMEBODY! . . . SOMEBODY! . . ." Ordinarily I would not visit a patient in a psychiatric ward without first discussing the situation with the psychiatrist. But as I paused just for a moment outside the door, the boy saw me and said questioningly, "Doctor? Sir?"

I stepped inside the room. "I'm not a doctor; I'm a minister," I said.

He repeated his question. "Doctor? Sir?" and then he added piteously, "Am I sunk? Am I done for?"

"No," I said gently, "You're not done for. God loves you, and you are going to get well."

Following a quiet prayer in which I invoked God's peace and comfort to surround him night and day, I took my leave. . . .

Sometimes I wake up in the night and still hear that same call . . . from people in every condition, whether of high or low degree, there come the echoes from around the globe—"SOMEBODY!"[26]

The prayer with the teenager was Dad's last ministerial function in St. Louis. He left the next day.

# Chapter 8

# National Council of Churches

*Some see the National Council of Churches as a plot to weaken the nation and the church. Others see it as a means for churches to cooperate in worldwide mission while preserving their individuality.*

When the general secretary of the National Council of Churches (NCC) first told Dad in May 1957 that he was being considered for the NCC presidency, Dad laughed it off, discounting the possibility entirely. In June, however, he received a long-distance call from the nominating committee saying that their choice was unanimous and asking if he would accept. Dad asked for time to discuss it with Emilie and with the chairpersons of the Delmar Church boards since it would require sacrifice on his wife's part and more work for the lay leaders of the church. As Dad prayed about his own doubts, the words of James Russell Lowell's hymn "Once to Every Man and Nation" came to his mind:

> Then to side with truth is noble, when we share her wretched crust,
> Ere her cause bring fame and profit, and 'tis prosperous to be just;
> Then it is the brave man chooses while the coward stands aside,
> Till the multitude make virtue of the faith they had denied.[1]

With all consultants in agreement with his sense of where God was leading, Dad accepted the challenge.

Being elected leader of the country's largest association of Protestant churches was a newsworthy event, particularly since Dad was the first ever to take the post while still actively pastoring a church. When the news broke, he was immediately in the national spotlight, sought by interviewers from *Time, Newsweek,* newspapers, radio, and national TV. He had great feelings of inadequacy and fears of temptation to self-importance. He need not have worried. He received enough encouragement and support from many church sources to overcome his doubts—and enough abuse and criticism from others to counteract any temptation.

A few months after starting his three-year term as president of the National Council of Churches, Dad began an address to the 1958 American Baptist Convention in Cincinnati with this story:

> Down in the State of Tennessee there were three rather disreputable characters who went by the name of the Johnson brothers. One night when coming home late from a party over in the next county, they stole a pig from a farmer's hog pen. Speeding down the highway for home, they heard a broadcast on the radio saying that one of Bill Cornpone's pigs had been stolen, and that roadblocks had been thrown up on every road in the county to stop the thieves from getting away. The Johnson brothers immediately stopped the car and went into conference. They decided they would disguise the pig as one of the neighbor boys and put him right in the front seat between two of the Johnson brothers, while the third brother sat in the back. So they put an overcoat on the pig with the collar up to his ears, pushed a felt hat down over his eyes . . . and then pulled a blanket up to his chin. Thus settled, they drove confidently on.
>
> Pretty soon they got to the roadblock. One of the highway patrol officers leaned in through the driver's open window, flashed his light around the inside of the car, and said, "Who are you boys?" "We're the Johnson brothers," was the reply. "O.K.," said the officer, "you there in the back seat—what's your name?" "George Johnson." "And you here at the wheel?" "Harry Johnson." "And the next guy?" "Oink!" said the pig. "Over there by the window—your name Johnson, too?" asked the officer. "Right," said the last of the passengers. "—Joe, that's me."
>
> "That's all," said the officer, "drive along."
>
> Later as the officer was reporting the incident to some of his fellow officers, he said, "But you know, that one brother, Oink Johnson, was one of the queerest looking characters I ever met!"
>
> Ever since I became president of the National Council of Churches, and have been right up in the middle of the front seat, I have had the uneasy feeling that maybe I am Oink Johnson. Because if I am to believe all the anonymous letters, pamphlets, and questions coming to me from as far away as Alaska and Hawaii, I am not only in disreputable company but am wearing a Communist coat, with a modernistic ecumenical blanket up to my chin, and a porkpie cloak-and-dagger hat pulled clear down over my shifty eyes and porcine snout.[2]

His first visit to the NCC headquarters in New York was typically low key. He browsed around, acquainting himself with the duties of the many employees. After several trips on the elevator, he introduced himself to the elevator operator: "I'm Dr. Dahlberg, the new president here."

"Well, I was sure you were the new president," said the elevator operator as he shook hands, "but that man who just got off, he said you were the new head electrician."

"He wasn't too far off at that," Dad reflected with a smile later. "Whenever there's a dim bulb in some department or someone blows a fuse, I'm called in."[3]

The National Council of the Churches of Christ in the USA, to give it its full name, was conceived as an association of church denominations. Its aim is cooperative effort in evangelism, study of world problems as they pertain to Christianity, and discussion of points of theology on which it might be possible to agree. It is not, and was never intended to be, a superchurch, and its pronouncements are not binding on its member denominations.[4] In the late 1950s, it numbered about thirty-six Protestant and Greek Orthodox denominations in the United States, with a membership of about thirty-nine million.

Since its beginning, the National Council had been held suspect by political and religious conservatives, with some claiming that it was a Communist front whose purpose was to take over America. Depending on who was talking, the NCC was pro-Jewish, pro-Arab, pro-Catholic, pro-Protestant, atheistic, liberal, Bible-destroying, unpatriotic, and a number of other adjectives. Many individual churches among the cooperating groups, including some American Baptists, refused to support it. Certain sections of the Lutheran Church, many evangelical churches, and the whole Southern Baptist Convention would have nothing to do with it, disavowing any ties of brotherhood with its affiliated church groups. Dad accepted this, saying that it was a good thing to have several groups on the outside offering criticism from time to time, to keep the NCC's feet on the ground.

Edwin T. Dahlberg, who gave a higher priority to God than to politics, caused a national furor. This was the aftermath of the McCarthy era, when Russia and Red China were the enemy and Communists were suspected to be hiding behind every bush.[5] Dad readily acknowledged that the Communist dictatorships of the USSR (Union of Soviet Socialist Republics) and China were contrary to both Christian doctrine and to democracy. It was only six years since his friend Henry Lin, president of Shanghai University, had been executed by the Chinese Communist government. As a former member of the Central Committee of the World Council of Churches (WCC), Dad had been kept well informed about conditions behind the Iron Curtain, "conditions [of persecution] like something out of the New Testament," as he put it. But in his initial address as president of the NCC, Dad firmly stated his belief that war was not the answer.

The Pentagon had recently responded to the threat of Soviet nuclear missiles with a promise of "massive retaliation." Dad countered that the gospel of Christ knows nothing of retaliation. Jesus' "point-four program" in the Sermon on the Mount was to love, to bless, to do good, and to pray; his church is under obligation, not to respond with massive retaliation but with massive *reconciliation* throughout the total life of mankind: "It is not half so important that we send Sputniks [the nickname given to the first orbiting satellite, launched that year by the Russians] circling the globe as that we send more loaves of bread around the world. It is the hunger and misery of the vast populations of the earth, the unrestrained birth rates, the production of military hardware, the fanatical ignorance and illiteracy of oppressed peoples that makes for war."[6]

The phrase "massive reconciliation" became a focus for both liberals and conservatives. Many missed the point and, instead of seeing a conflict between the teachings of the gospel and the national policy of the day, made it a question of patriotism.

Dad agreed with his predecessor, Eugene Carson Blake, who had stated that the United States should study diplomatic recognition of Communist China. It was ridiculous to ignore the existence of one-fifth of the human race, Dad said, and furthermore the situation was no different from that of Russia, which the U.S. did recognize. This view elicited the anger not only of many Americans but also of President Chiang Kai-shek of Nationalist China, Red China's principal foe. Chiang pointedly was unavailable when Dad later made a visit to Taiwan. It was to be some fifteen years before Republican President Richard Nixon proposed, and accomplished, the diplomatic recognition of China.

Sometimes the reception of a pronouncement depends upon who makes it. Consider, for example: "Every gun that is made, every warship launched, every rocket fired, signifies, in the final sense, a theft from those who hunger and are not fed, those who are cold and not clothed. This is not a way of life at all. . . . Under the cloud of threatening war, it is humanity hanging from a cross of iron."[7]

This is just the type of statement that would cause conservatives to damn the head of the National Council of Churches if the president had indeed uttered it. Although Dad would have fully agreed with such a statement, it is actually a quotation from President Eisenhower, former commander of Allied Forces in Europe, who uttered it five years before Dad became NCC president. There were, no doubt, some who would object to such a thought expressed by anyone, but there were not many who seriously thought Eisenhower a threat to the country's security.

Dad firmly held that one could be both a pacifist and a patriot. Invited to speak at a meeting of Protestant churches of northern New York at Plattsburgh Air Base in 1959, he chose as his topic "The Protestant Contribution to Patriotism," which he cited as (1) religious liberty, (2) an educated citizenry, and (3) a biblical faith.[8] It was well received by the large audience, by the local press, and by his military hosts, but it did not placate many of his critics.

Of course, dissension and criticism drew the most attention in the news media. Though Dad acknowledged this, he felt it personally sometimes, even when it was bizarre. "Today I got a letter addressed to Dear Satan," he wrote in a family letter in 1959. "It was from some fellow down in Texas, protesting my having written some Lenten season editorials for the Associated Press. The man said that Lent and Easter were pagan festivals, and a Christian had no business having anything to do with them. . . . When they begin calling a guy Satan it is about as low as he can get."[9]

Despite the attacks, Dad kept his eyes on the goal of reconciliation. Difference of opinion was acceptable; responding in kind to hate mail and public attacks was not. The next week he was in Corpus Christi, Texas, addressing a state meeting of the United Church Women and reported in a letter: "I had an open forum after the meeting, plus a session with about a dozen oilmen, geologists, lawyers and others who were worried about the social gospel emphasis of the National Council. We had a fine time, and it helped to clarify things."[10] And in one of his 1960 letters he observed, "This afternoon I leave for Jacksonville, Florida, for three addresses tomorrow—two at the University and the other at the annual meeting of the Florida Council of Churches. The Ministers' Association in Jacksonville has protested against the Episcopal Church opening its pulpit to me, but I am used to this by now, and don't let it bother me. I am having breakfast with the dissenters in the morning."[11]

Not only did Dad work for grassroots cooperation, but he spoke with national leaders when opportunity arose. In October of 1958, there was a cornerstone-laying ceremony for the new Interchurch Center in New York City. Dad and Mother attended, along with Mr. and Mrs. McCarthy of Delmar Church (Mrs. McCarthy representing the World YWCA). Dad, Eugene Carson Blake, President Kirk of Columbia University, and President Eisenhower stood on the steps of New York's Riverside Church (next to the new building site) and reviewed a procession of choirs, clergy, flags, and academic representatives as they marched by in the brilliant October sunshine, amidst a throng of thirty thousand people stretching as far as Grant's Tomb. Following several addresses, President Eisenhower laid the cornerstone, splashing some cement on his suit as he did so and joining in the laughter as someone remarked to the stonemasons standing by, "That's what you get for letting a non-union man help you."[12]

After the ceremony, accompanied by six Secret Service men, Dr. Blake and Dad rode with the president to LaGuardia Airport, preceded by two carloads of Secret Service agents and thirty motorcycle police plus more Secret Service and police following. Crowds lined the streets and overpasses to see the president and point him out to their children. Although President Eisenhower waved and smiled at the crowds, he also took time to speak to the two church leaders at length about the Far East situation as they rode. A two-week extension of the cease-fire between Red China and the offshore islands had been announced that afternoon.[13] A pleased Eisenhower told Dad and Blake that he believed this would mean a continuing and indefinite extension of the cease-fire, without any official commitment on America's part. Eisenhower believed that the United States had no business in Quemoy but also that Chiang Kai-shek "is a very difficult man to deal with. He is deeply religious, to the extent that he will even withdraw from a long conference to pray. And when you get a stubborn man who is religious about it, you have a real problem on your hands." (Presumably this oblique comment on religious people was not lost on his two-man audience.) The president believed that from a military point of view, the value of Quemoy and the Matsus (islands in the straits between Taiwan and China) was very small, but Chiang had put a third of his army in there just the same, involving the U.S. deeply. Eisenhower told the two, "I'd give my right arm to know the answer [to this dilemma]."[14]

Returning to the subject of the Interchurch Center, Eisenhower was enthusiastic, saying to Dad, "I'm really nuts about this matter of the Protestant churches getting together." He quoted a proverb of his mother's: "God deals out the cards, but he expects us to play them."

September 1959 brought another opportunity for conversation with the president when a delegation of one hundred NCC leaders met with Eisenhower and presented to him the National Council Peace Study Program, which was to be launched in all the participating church denominations later in the year. "As spokesman for the delegation," wrote Dad,

"I had the pleasant experience of having five or ten minutes with the president alone, in his office, along with HEW [Department of Health, Education, and Welfare] Secretary Fleming. During this brief session the president asked a number of questions about the National Council and about our peace program, which I hope I answered helpfully, and he told me something about Khrushchev's visit coming up this week." The president then met with the whole delegation, after which the NCC leaders had a two-hour briefing from State Department leaders on various trouble spots in the world. "Altogether, it was a great day," wrote Dad, "not only because we met with the president, but also in the consolidation of our ecumenical forces. We have never had such a representative delegation before. Some came from the West Coast, others from Europe, to be present."[15]

President Eisenhower's invitation to USSR premier Nikita Khrushchev had met with mixed reaction from the American people. Some had proposed that everyone should wear black armbands of mourning and that air-raid sirens and church bells sound a warning wherever Khrushchev appeared. Dad acknowledged that little would be achieved by showing a tough, ruthless enemy some model farms and factories or by having pleasant conversations, but he nevertheless pointed out advantages to the encounter:

> Two things are to be remembered. Khrushchev will have a chance to see democracy at work, and to learn that we are not a decadent slave people withering on the vine. Furthermore, we should remember that after Khrushchev's visit here, President Eisenhower will be going to Russia. The Iron Curtain will be lifted just a little. The people of Asia and Africa will have an opportunity to get more of the truth about us, and we will have an opportunity to learn more of the truth about conditions in Russia. To keep the avenues of communication open in this way is the world's greatest hope for peace.[16]

In any event, of course, it was Khrushchev's pounding his shoe on Russia's desk in the UN General Assembly that captured the nation's attention and emphasized his nature better than any black armbands could have done.

As observers of the Protestant scene are aware, the arguments for and against the National Council of Churches have continued for many years beyond Dad's tenure. Thirty years later, a denomination's membership in the National Council would be automatic grounds for exclusion from full membership in the National Association of Evangelical Churches of America (NAE). (Although dual membership is still not accepted by the

NAE, fraternal "observers" from NCC member churches are welcome at their conventions.) But there has been occasional cooperative work. In 1959, Dad was one of a group of representatives of the NCC who went to Puerto Rico to help the National Council of Evangelical Churches of Puerto Rico develop a program of cooperative Christianity. And after the presidential election in 1960, there was an informal conference in Washington, attended not only by NCC members but by Southern Baptists, Missouri Synod Lutherans, and members of the NAE, to assess political fallout from the election.[17]

On the trip to Puerto Rico, which occurred the year before the Kennedy-Nixon presidential election, two questions predominated during media or student interviews. One was about the pope's proposal for holding an ecumenical council; the other, about the possibility of a Roman Catholic president of the United States.

Regarding the former, Dad told the press that although he welcomed any friendly step toward Christian unity, Protestants had not yet been invited to attend or have any part in planning the pope's ecumenical council. If an invitation came, he continued, it would have to be evaluated on the basis of equality and freedom issues, for Protestants did not accept the authority of the pope, the union of church and state, and the extreme veneration of the Virgin Mary.

In response to the second question, Dad acknowledged that there is nothing in the Constitution to prevent a Roman Catholic from becoming president, but several questions do arise: What would be his stand on the appointment of an American ambassador to the Vatican? What would be his position on the use of public tax funds for Roman Catholic parochial schools? What would be his attitude towards the separation of church and state? Would he support or veto legislation pertaining to [preconception] birth control? "It isn't in any sense bigotry nor intolerance to want these questions clarified," said Dad; "we should ask them of a Protestant candidate, too. Our religious freedom is important."[18] (In the election the following year Dad voted for Kennedy, apparently satisfied with the candidate's statements in the interim. Mother voted for Nixon. That's democracy.)

## Christmas Ministry to the Armed Forces

The attitude of U.S. military leaders toward Edwin T. Dahlberg was something of a paradox. On the one hand, the Pentagon probably did not care to have a pacifist speaking out against their policies, even though the

Selective Service System (military draft) had always provided exemption from military duty for those who objected to war on religious grounds. On the other hand, military leaders recognized the need for providing religious counsel for members of the armed forces and had an extensive corps of military chaplains for that purpose. As head of the largest Protestant organization in the United States, Dahlberg was acknowledged as a religious leader of high rank. Accordingly, he was invited by the military to spend the 1957 Christmas season visiting the armed forces in the Far North.

Dad accepted gladly. He saw no conflict with his pacifist views. These were young men and women of the armed forces, far from home and in need of spiritual support, just as his church's two hundred servicemen and servicewomen had been during the war. On the shortest day of the year, therefore, with the sun setting at 2:41 P.M., Dad disembarked at Elmendorf Air Force Base outside Anchorage, Alaska. This was his first visit to Alaska, and his letters express his enthusiasm:

> Being officially listed as a VIP, I have the use of General Armstrong's plane during my entire stay. He is head of the entire Alaskan Command, including the Army, Navy, Air Force, DEW Line stations, etc. It is a beautiful plane, a four-engine job; the two pilots, Major Gay and Major Allen, are really experts. . . . I spend much time in the cockpit with them, as it is so interesting to watch them at the controls, and there is at the same time such a magnificent panorama of the Alaskan landscape.
>
> Colonel Poch, the chief chaplain of the Alaskan Command, and Don Bolles, public relations man for the National Council, are always along on these trips. Colonel Poch arranges all the schedules and Don handles all the press releases. This matter of press relations is very important, as Fulton Lewis, John Flynn, and Dr. [Carl] McIntire, all of whom went after Bishop Oxnam so hard some years ago, are now making such savage attacks on me as a communist, a red, etc.—an indirect way of trying to discredit the National Council. The New York tabloid, *The Mirror,* even had a picture of me the other night, on the front page, side by side with [one of] Victor Scobell, the convicted spy—a kind of guilt by association picture. This has been printed and reported all over Alaska this week, but Don said that although some of the military here had had some anxious moments in advance of my coming, they have been completely won over. Certainly they have given me a most cordial and warm-hearted welcome at every point, with all the top generals and officers giving dinners and receptions of the highest order, and extending every courtesy, even though I have spoken my deepest convictions. The enlisted personnel, and their wives and children, seem to be profoundly grateful for our coming, many of them being quite homesick and lonesome at this time of the year.[19]

 Despite his pacifism, Dad had many words of praise for the ability and the efficiency of the Air Force, as he watched airmen scrambling in a simulated "red alert": "The whole organization of the Alaskan Command is a magnificent evidence of American courage and power, but I still do not think this is the real way to defend the nation. Some day, I am afraid, some nervous finger is going to trigger off the whole business, and we will have fireworks exploding all over the world in a war of total destruction."[20]

One thing Dad could not get used to was military protocol. He was the VIP everywhere he went, with protocol rank equal to major general or rear admiral,[21] and nobody could leave a reception or dinner until he had turned to shake hands with the general and the general's wife and excused himself. Only then could the rest go home and go to bed. Dad was never one to cut short his conversation when visiting at the church door after a service, and he really had to watch himself so that he would not delay everyone: "It would do . . . Emilie an immense amount of good to see me in this predicament, as she knows all too well my proclivities for visiting." It also bemused the family (and probably many of Dad's detractors, too) to see newspaper photographs of him debarking from an Air Force plane to review his honor guard of marines, but it did not faze him.

Dad's tour in 1957 was such a success that the military asked him back each Christmas of his NCC tenure. In the Christmas season of 1958, he, with thirty clergy, toured Strategic Air Command Headquarters at Nebraska's Offut Air Force Base, with its underground command post for America's bomber squadrons. Dad then flew overseas by commercial plane to Spain, visiting American bases at Torrejon and Zaragoza, and went on to the U.S. Naval Air Station at Port Lyautey in Morocco, visiting personnel and their families at each base. He landed at Port Lyautey at the tail end of a hurricane that had left eight hundred square miles of Morocco under water and four thousand people homeless. Going with naval officers to the scene, Dad and his party were met by the district governor. He was able to tell the governor that Church World Service (the relief arm of the NCC) had, that morning, sent $2,000 to help the people of his district. Through an interpreter, the governor expressed his appreciation. Lieutenant Commander Blair, a naval officer fluent in Arabic and in charge of the relief operations, said that this $2,000 would be worth $20,000,000 in Moroccan goodwill towards the people of the United States.[22]

The tour at Christmas of 1959 was of military bases at Guam, Okinawa, Taiwan, and the Philippines. In Taiwan, Dad and his WCC public relations companion, Dr. Bushmeyer, encountered a very hostile press and much bitterness among the Taiwanese pastors and American missionaries. Fundamentalist groups in Taiwan had presented their own view of the Cleveland conference (where the NCC had advocated study of possible Red China admission to the UN). The Taiwanese press wanted an interview on Red China from Dad, but army officials hurried him on past them. He had dinner that evening with pastors, missionaries, and government representatives, including Acting American Ambassador Yaeger. The assemblage questioned Dad intensely, though always courteously. Some of the questioners contended that total nuclear annihilation of the human race was preferable to any kind of cooperation with Red China. (Looking back on the scene from a generation later, we should remember that China was equally unreasonable in its public attitude toward the West and that implausible statements were made on both sides.) One asked Dad if he would support admission of Red China to the United Nations, and when he replied that he would, there was an immediate and general exclamation of "God forbid!"[23]

Dad and Bushmeyer found themselves very much isolated from the civilian community, and Taiwan President Chiang Kai-shek canceled a scheduled meeting with them without comment. The American military was more cordial, and Christmas services at Linkai Security Base were well received. One southern woman told Dad enthusiastically, "You preach just like an old-time Methodist. We don't hear many of them these days!" Dad went on to Okinawa to visit many of the bases under the command of Marine General Luckey and Air Force General Smith, both of whom he greatly respected. Sixty thousand servicemen, including thirty-five thousand marines, were stationed on Okinawa at the time. He visited a tank battalion at Camp Hanson, a small Coast Guard station five miles off the coast at Ike-Shima, a Nike missile installation, a military hospital, Naha Air Base, and several camps of Marines, speaking or leading Christmas services for the personnel and their families.[24] Dad also met with the unit chaplains at every opportunity and hoped his meetings with the commanding generals would strengthen the chaplain programs.

He was asked to make a fourth Christmas tour—this time of Caribbean bases—in 1960, but he declined. It was his last week in the NCC post, and Dad felt he owed some Christmas time to Delmar Church.

Throughout Dad's NCC ministry, and particularly after viewing America's military might at close hand, he spoke out on the futility of atomic warfare: "There is a strong feeling that we must adopt some non-military approaches to peace if we are going to break the present stalemate. This would involve more intelligent economic aid, technical assistance, medical care, literacy programs, as well as a more vigorous religious approach to the needs of the world. I thoroughly agree with [Catholic] Bishop Fulton J. Sheen that the ultimate hope of mankind lies within the dimensions of religion."[25]

## A Wider Audience

When the general board of the NCC met in Hartford, Connecticut, in February of 1959, Dad made one of his most widely quoted addresses. "The Churches and the National Conscience" was broadcast over all New England and reported in the next day's *New York Times:*

> Jesus did not confine himself to so-called matters of comfort, peace of mind, and family conduct, but spoke out on the public questions of the day: Samaritan segregation, the temple tax, tribute to Caesar, and Roman conscription.
>
> It was because he entered so vigorously into controversial areas that Jesus went to the cross. If he had dealt only with little Mickey Mouse morals, he never would have been heard of. We have a Biblical mandate to enlighten the conscience of our generation on the life and death issues of our day, [among] which are those pertaining to economics, race relations, peace and war, separation of Church and State.[26]

His speaking schedule increased greatly as his term in the NCC went on. He was away from home more nights than not, and he welcomed the beginning in 1959 of commercial jet plane service, which cut much of his travel time in half. His audiences spanned the whole spectrum of American life. He addressed three thousand United Steelworkers, "a more rough and tumble lot than the Baptists even," but confessed in a letter that he did not choose wage disputes as his topic: "Only once in my life have I ever had the courage to preach on John the Baptist's advice 'Be content with your wages,' and that was mostly directed at new seminary graduates."[27]

The week after addressing the Steelworkers, he was in Philadelphia for two addresses to the Society of Friends (the Quakers), on to Wabash, Indiana, to meet with five hundred Methodist laypeople, then back to St. Louis to speak at a conference of Women in Radio and TV and to address eighteen hundred delegates of the International Association of Public School Officials. This was only a slightly busier than usual week for him, and the more places he spoke, the more the number of invitations seemed to multiply.[28]

The Boy Scout Jamboree in Colorado Springs in 1960 furnished Dad the biggest live audience of his career. Fifty-six thousand boys were registered at the encampment, and thirty-six thousand of them attended the united Protestant Sunday morning worship service. "Including the Catholic, Jewish, Mormon, Quaker, and Buddhist services, attendance was almost 100 percent, even though all the services were voluntary," he wrote. "It was a great sight to see the boys marching to church in columns two, four, and eight abreast, some of the columns being two miles long, coming from all directions, with Pikes Peak as a backdrop. It was the experience of a lifetime for me, and I guess for the boys, with all the programs celebrating the 50th year of Scouting. I spoke on 'High Altitude Religion.'"[29] In the sermon, he told the Scouts of his experiences climbing some of Colorado's highest mountain peaks, where the world is "clean, clear, and close to God." As usual, Dad received some bizarre criticism along with the excitement:

> A lady called up just a few minutes ago and asked if I had a copy of my speech, as she would like to have one. I told her I had sent my only extra copy to the National Scout headquarters for press releases. "Well," she said, "I would like to see one. I know you are president of a Communist organization, and that your speech to the Scouts will be slanted toward Communism." Then she hung up. I sure get my patience tested sometimes. On the cheerful side, however, was a strong editorial in the Southern Baptist *Texas Standard,* defending the National Council. Now that these wild-eyed propagandists are charging the Southern Baptists with being soft on Communism, our brethren in Dixie are beginning to realize a little better than they did what we have been up against all these years.[30]

During the whole three years that he was NCC president, Dad continued his work as pastor of Delmar Baptist Church in St. Louis even though he was on the road most of each week. Delmar Church was very tolerant of their senior pastor's busy schedule outside the church and did everything they could to ease the tremendous burden of correspondence, speeches, and travel that he had. The assistant pastor, Larry Loughhead, took over much of the pastoral visits to members in need and some of the Sunday preaching, and the church hired an extra secretary during the three years Dad headed the NCC. The only protest from the church staff was after Dad had an interview in the magazine *Parade,* which brought in such a flood of correspondence that the secretaries pleaded half seriously, "Please, Dr. Dahlberg, no more interviews!"

Dad felt a great obligation to look after the church as his basic task and, whenever possible, arranged the speaking engagements to avoid weekends and major church meetings. As in his other earlier churches, he occasionally held evangelistic visitation nights, with forty or more members visiting those who had expressed interest in the church or in Christianity. He led an annual planning retreat for the church, spent time with individual members, and preached at Sunday worship on most Sundays. His commitment to the church is revealed in a 1959 letter he wrote to me:

> Today I was going to put in a whole day of writing articles and speeches that have been long overdue, but had to spend the entire day working on the case of one of our high school boys who got into bad trouble last night by breaking into a dog and cat hospital and taking some money. He is out on bail now, but I am afraid it will go hard with him. His father and mother are wonderful people, and simply heartbroken over it. What kids won't do! Of all the places to break into I should think a dog and cat hospital would be the last place one would think of. All the watch dogs . . .

## The Air Force Manual

A major story involving the NCC hit the national press in early 1960. When the NCC general board met in Oklahoma City in February 1960, it confronted startling newspaper headlines:

AIR FORCE MANUAL TIES COMMIES TO CHURCHES
Capitol Aides Stunned. Use Halted.[31]

Air Training Command Headquarters at Lackland Air Force Base in Texas used the manual in question to train noncommissioned officers of the Air Force Reserve in security matters. Sixty-one hundred copies were printed and 3,290 distributed to training centers around the United States before Air Force Secretary Dudley Sharp ordered the manual withdrawn, promising a full-scale inquiry to determine the responsible parties.[32]

Most of the manual was straightforward instruction in the posting of guards, security maintenance, personnel recognition, and so on. One section, however, informed the trainee,

> Communists and Communist fellow-travelers and sympathizers have successfully infiltrated our churches. The foregoing is not an isolated example, by any means; it is known that even the pastors of certain of our churches are

card-carrying Communists! The extent of Communistic activities in religious groups is further detailed below. . . . The National Council of Churches of Christ in the U.S.A. officially sponsored the Revised Standard Version of the Bible. Of the 95 persons who served on this project, 30 have been affiliated with pro-Communist fronts, projects, and publications.[33]

The irate public relations department of the NCC immediately contacted the secretaries of the Defense Department and of the Air Force.The manual, however, had more to say: "Another rather foolish remark often heard is that Americans have a right to know what's going on. Most people realize the foolhardiness of such a suggestion. If a football team should start telling the other side the plays it planned to use, their opponents would sweep them off the field."[34]

This remark angered the nation's press and universities, who saw a difference between protecting military strategy and the insertion of unproven political statements in a military training manual. Telegrams of support from educators and editors poured into NCC headquarters. The *Washington Post* published a cartoon of an Air Force commander bowed in discouragement at his desk, with a list of crack-ups on the wall beside him. An airman is shown coming in and saying, "Chalk up another one, Chief. This time we hit a church."[35]

"I had to turn the chair over to the vice-presidents two or three times," wrote Dad of the NCC meeting in Oklahoma, "while I went out and answered questions of the reporters. One day I had three TV cameras and eight reporters focused on me at one time, which doesn't make it any easier to keep a clear head. I hope I came out of it with credit to the Council, however. In the meantime, we have had flocks of telegrams from all over the country, pledging support to our cause."[36]

The debate in Congress two months later, on 19 April 1960, did much to swing public opinion in favor of the NCC.[37] Congressman John E. Moss (D-Calif.) termed the manual an outrageous display of arrogance. Senator Prescott Bush (R-Conn.) called the use of such a manual incredibly stupid. The House of Representatives spent much of three days discussing the matter, mostly favorable to the National Council. (Many of the members of the House belonged to church denominations that participated in the NCC, and even if they themselves did not, they knew that large numbers of constituents did.) Congresswoman Green of Oregon addressed the House on religious freedom, quoting letters from many constituents back home. She pointed out that the writer of the manual, a man with long experience in writing manuals for the Army and Air Force, had admitted later that he had doubts about the propriety of the subject in a Defense Department manual. Congressman Brademas (D) of Indiana cited the *Indianapolis Star*'s editorial defense of the manual but countered it with quotations from another ten nationally prominent city newspapers that denounced the Air Force's carelessness in not questioning or verifying the material it had printed, nor even consulting its own office of chaplains for comment. Both Brademas and Congressman Schwengel of Iowa listed the activities, departments, budget, and functions of the NCC in great detail, and Schwengel inserted a two-page biography of NCC President Dahlberg into the record.

Congressman Walter (D-Penn.), however, the chairman of the House Un-American Affairs Committee, defended the manual and asserted his belief that the charges of Communism were true since the NCC supported diplomatic recognition of Red China. Brademas replied that he was, himself, opposed to recognition of China, but that did not make Communists of those holding the opposite view. Congressman Johnson of Colorado pointed out that the Revised Standard Version of the Bible was not a Communist-inspired document merely because it updated the language of the King James Version (published in 1611), adding that the King James had also been denounced as blasphemy by some church leaders during its first century of use.

Several fundamentalist groups habitually at odds with the NCC, and which claimed many times that the NCC was aiding a Communist takeover of America, objected to any apology from the Air Force.[38] Tulsa radio/TV evangelist Billy James Hargis claimed responsibility for the allegations in the Air Force manual, according to the *Minneapolis Tribune*.[39] Posting placards around the city that said, "*We* dare. Does *He* dare?" Hargis challenged Dad to a public debate in the Oklahoma City Auditorium.[40] Dad declined since the Air Force had withdrawn the manual and apologized and since the NCC did not want to give further publicity to the opposing groups.

In June, Hargis and a staff of eight people, including secretaries, newspaper consultants, radio announcers and technicians, plus his wife, three children, and a nurse, came to St. Louis, staying in the Ambassador Hotel. His purpose was to lecture on "Betrayed in Government, in the Schools, and in the Pulpit." Dad's secretary, Lois Brackman, went to hear him and "got her blood pressure up to such a point she could hardly settle down to dictation."[41] Pleased as Dad had been with the outcome of the Air Force manual investigation, he felt that there was still one more aspect to address:

reconciliation was more important than victory. The main object in conflict is not, he said, "Win the victory and eliminate the enemy," but "Win the enemy and eliminate the enmity." Against all advice he made a phone call.

Hargis's secretary picked up the phone in the hotel suite, and his eyes must have widened in incredulity. Dad could hear him informing his employer, "Some phoney is on the phone who says he's Dahlberg of the National Council of Churches!" The Oklahoma evangelist took the phone, skepticism changing to amazement and then to wary acceptance of Dad's invitation to lunch at the University Club.[42]

"Hargis turned out to be a pretty good egg," wrote Dad. "I don't think I converted him to the National Council, but I believe we had a very worthwhile session. We sat and talked for four hours together, and at the end of it I said, 'Let's just have a time of prayer together.' I prayed, and at the end of it Hargis said, 'I promise you now, I will never again say a harsh word about you!' And he never did."[43, 44]

Another episode of conflict happened at the 1960 convention of the American Baptists—Dad's own denomination—in Rochester, New York. A delegation from a church in Kansas brought a resolution urging severing relations with the National Council of Churches for being modernist and soft on Communism. The convention delegates voted it down three thousand to fifty. "It was not alone the numerical result that was so pleasing," wrote Dad, "but the resounding enthusiasm with which the action was taken. It was so decisive that the critics of the Council were surprised and chagrined. They had completely underestimated the strength of ecumenical sentiment."[45]

## Recognition and Condemnation

During Dad's term as president, the National Council of Churches distributed millions of dollars in relief programs such as CROP, One Great Hour of Sharing, and Church World Service. He was instrumental in the NCC's policy of refusing to hold meetings where racial minorities were not welcomed. And during his tenure, the NCC dedicated its new nineteen-story office building, New York City's Interchurch Center. He told me later, "If all our church people in the United States could see it, I think they would quickly realize that the National Council of Churches is something more than an Air Force Manual argument."[46]

Dad had personal accomplishments at this time as well. He received his third and fourth honorary doctor's degrees,[47] the Gandhi Peace

Award,[48] and induction into the Otoe Indian tribe as an honorary chieftain with the name Waconda Geloukhee— "Preacher of the Great Spirit."

He also had become accustomed to enduring personal insults in the media as well as face-to-face. While attending a meeting in Little Rock just before integration of the schools there, he was confronted with a group bearing placards, "Edwin T. Dahlberg—Atheist! Communist! Integrationist!"[49] In many cities he was accused of being a traitor, or at best a dupe of the Communists. But in serving God, reconciliation was always his business. Any measure that reduced hostility or brought about peace, any understanding in the hearts of two opposing sides, any smoothing of the road by which an individual might come to know Christ, helped accomplish his goal.

The last week of the year 1960 marked the end of Dad's three-year term as well as his sixty-eighth birthday and the tenth anniversary of his pastorate in St. Louis. The church gave him a surprise party in celebration of all three and presented him with a fake telegram that read: "Rejoicing over the completion of your tenure as National Council President. Glad to see you leave the national scene. Signed, Billy James Hargis, Carl McIntire, United States Air Force, Fulton Lewis Jr., and Emilie."[50]

## Opposition to NCC Continues

"I have gotten into the eye of another church storm, much against my will," Dad wrote in September 1961. "Three weeks from now I am scheduled to give three addresses at the Ohio Baptist Convention at the Linden Avenue Baptist Church in Columbus, but the church has withdrawn its invitation to the convention because of my being on the program. This has been because of the agitation of a Bible Baptist church in Columbus, plus the pressure of the John Birch Society, and a threat by an insurance company to discharge two of the members of the church unless my coming is canceled."[51] The Ohio Baptists reemphasized their desire to have Dad come and changed the place of meeting to the First Baptist Church of Columbus.

In a family letter, Dad explained, "I offered to step out of the picture, as I certainly don't want to be the cause of any division either in the convention or in the Linden Avenue church. It's a puzzle to me how a peaceful, noncontroversial guy like me always seems to become such a bone of contention—never in my own church, but among people I have never seen nor known."

"This is going to be something like Daniel going into the lions' den," Dad commented two weeks later, "except that the Lord stopped the mouths of the lions, whereas I have to face a two-hour open forum with no holds barred." First Baptist of Columbus took a vote whether to host the convention in the face of mounting pressure from the Birch Society, the Circuit Riders, and other concerned conservatives and reaffirmed the invitation by a vote of 61 percent to 39 percent. Dad again offered to withdraw, figuring that the outcome was certainly less-than-overwhelming affirmation, but the convention program committee said that withdrawal would complicate matters still further and probably would cause cancellation of the whole convention. "I guess I am in for about the biggest test I have ever faced," Dad went on. "My prayer is that God will so enable me to conduct myself that it might all turn out to us as a testimony, as Christ promised." He was encouraged by the unswerving loyalty of his own church in St. Louis and many letters from Ohio assuring him of supporting prayers.[52]

The positive side of the conflict was that twice as many people attended the meetings as were expected, and the two-hour forum was rebroadcast on Columbus and Cleveland radio stations, creating a much wider audience for presenting the NCC's case. Police guarded the convention site that afternoon, and plainclothes officers were in the congregation, but the precautions proved unnecessary.

The Circuit Riders[53] had prepared a list of twenty-five questions they wanted Dad to answer. He, in turn, prepared a statement.[54] Before addressing their questions, he began by saying that he knew of no National Council leaders who had any Communist sympathies whatever and decried the propaganda of "professional controversialists" who implied that there were.

Nine of the Circuit Riders' twenty-five charges concerned Dad's signing petitions for the repeal of the McCarran Act.[55] Since both Democratic and Republican presidents, Truman and Eisenhower, had also urged repeal or major modification of it, Dad failed to see why the NCC president should be charged with Communist sympathies because of seeking its repeal.

Six other charges related to Dad's being a member of a sponsoring committee for a dinner at which Bishop Oxnam was honored by the Society for American-Soviet Friendship. Dad pointed out that the dinner was in 1943 when Russia and the U.S. were military allies and that it was attended not only by Bishop Oxnam but by Eleanor Roosevelt, John

Foster Dulles, Armed Forces Secretary Finletter, Secretary of State Stettinius, and most of the top political and military leaders of the U.S. General Eisenhower had also sent a cablegram expressing the hope that the dinner would further cement the alliance against Hitler. Dad called the singling out of Bishop Oxnam by the Circuit Riders false witness of the lowest order.

Seven more of the charges related to Dad's membership in the Fellowship of Reconciliation (FOR), which the Circuit Riders charged was a Communist front organization. The FOR's membership, Dad said, includes some of the most patriotic pastors and laypeople of America, and the organization is dedicated to one cause alone—international disarmament and world peace by nonviolent means, a cause that would not be tolerated in Communist Russia.

The last three charges concerned Dad's signing petitions. He acknowledged that if he had known in the 1930s and 1940s what he now knew about Harry Bridges and Earl Browder, he would not have asked for a review of their cases, although many American leaders of impeccable American patriotism had also signed. The third petition asked for a review of new evidence on behalf of Martin Sobell, who was at that time in prison. Dad, who had signed at the personal request of Mrs. Sobell, said he would ask for the same review on the behalf of any thief, drunkard, or murderer. Dad concluded by stating that he had been pastor of five different churches in the past forty-three years and that not one member of any of the congregations had ever questioned his loyalty as an American patriot. The thousand-member audience gave him a standing ovation at the end of the forum. Undaunted, representatives of the John Birch Society passed out their literature as the audience exited.[56]

This episode by no means ended the conflict between pro– and anti–National Council of Churches camps. The NCC continues to be a lightning rod in the debate over conservative and liberal values.[57] The allegation that the NCC was a Communist plot was largely defused by the election of an industrialist as Dad's successor, J. Irwin Miller, chairman of the Cummins Engineering Co., the largest U.S. manufacturer of diesel engines. The debate thereafter shifted more toward theological grounds, but there are still many churches, three decades later, where mention of the NCC is a flash point for heated discussion.

# Chapter 9

# The Vietnam War Years

*At the age of seventy, Edwin T. Dahlberg retired from actively pastoring a church. He taught young ministerial students for a couple of years, and then the Vietnam War came along. He supported the servicemen and servicewomen overseas, but like many of his compatriots, he found the conduct of the war incompatible with either the Christian or the American message.*

The original plan was to spend the retirement years in Rochester, New York, Mother's girlhood home, and where Dad was a trustee of his alma mater, Colgate Rochester Divinity School. Before they left St. Louis in early 1963, however, an invitation came that struck Dad and Mother as an attractive way to begin retirement. Crozer Seminary, in Chester, Pennsylvania, had an opening for a part-time professor to teach student ministers the skills of pastoring that are not usually learned from books. The seminary asked Dad whether he would accept the position for a three-year period, which he did with pleasure. He had always wanted to teach.

Crozer Seminary, in a suburb of Philadelphia, proved to be a restful change. Dad enjoyed lecturing the senior class two hours a week ("Preaching and Pastoral Ministry" the first semester, and "The Ecumenical Movement" the second).[1] He spent much time in counselling and in informal gatherings with the students.

## Interracial Relations

Martin Luther King Jr. had graduated from Crozer as class valedictorian in 1951, and Dad took renewed interest in this crusader for racial justice. Because of King's student years at Crozer, Dad liked to think of him as an American Baptist, at least by adoption, and they corresponded occasionally.

Dr. King had just given his "I Have a Dream" address in Washington (23 August 1963) when Dad began teaching at Crozer. In 1963, Dr. King was arrested in Alabama for his attempts to integrate some of Birmingham's public facilities. In his famous "Letter from Birmingham Jail," he chided white clergy who felt that his efforts were ill timed. "Asian and African nations are fast achieving independence," King told them, "while we still creep at a horse-and-buggy pace toward gaining a cup of coffee at a lunch counter."

To Dad, Dr. King wrote quite a different letter:

> Dear Dr. Dahlberg, For weeks I have been intending to write a few words to you to express my sincere appreciation for your consoling words that came to me in the form of a letter when I was in prison. All that you said served to give me new courage and vigor to carry on. I shall always be indebted to you for your moral support and concern. You ask where money might be sent for my defense. . . . [He then dealt with the details of that.] May God continue to bless you and all the great work you are doing.[2]

Dad had been fighting racial discrimination twenty-five years or more before the lunch-counter sit-ins in the South. My brother, Bruce, recalls an incident in the mid-1930s when our family was attending the Minnesota State Fair and stopped at a small food stand for hamburgers. A black couple sat down next to us and also placed an order. The waitress told them they would have to pay a dollar per item (this was in a time when the average hamburger cost fifteen to twenty-five cents). At that, the black couple got up to leave, but Dad rose and asked them to wait a moment. He turned to the waitress. "If you won't serve this couple, you won't serve us either," he told her. As we left, he gave the black couple his business card, and that was the end of it that afternoon. Some days later, however, the Minnesota secretary of state phoned Dad to tell him that the black man had showed Dad's card to his own pastor, who then contacted the office of the manager of the fairgrounds. The manager rescinded the food stand's fairground permit and closed it down.

Dad also had spoken to the problem in his inaugural address to the NCC in 1957:

> It is significant that this session of the National Council of Churches is meeting in St. Louis. This could not have happened three years ago. . . . Because the Assembly cannot be held in any city where the delegates of all races do not receive equal hospitality, we were not in a position to invite the National Council at that time. . . . There are still large areas of town where a non-white can buy a hamburger only if he eats it off the premises. That's the

trouble with our religion. We sing the hymn "Standing on the Promises of God," but we don't even want to catch a brother sitting on the premises. Or we sing "Whosoever Will May Come." Come where? To Christ? Yes! But not to the church, the school, the employment office, or the hotel. Such is the mixed up idea of our religion.[3]

In 1964, Mr. and Mrs. Victor Gavel, of Delmar Church, proposed and funded "The Dahlberg Peace Award," to be presented at each biennial convention of American Baptists "to the person or church who has done outstanding work for peace [defined as bringing reconciliation between persons, groups, and nations], with evidence of activity and solid accomplishment within the past three years." Except for his name, Dad had no function in making the award, whose recipients are chosen by a committee of Baptists. Its first recipient was Dr. Martin Luther King Jr.

By the end of his second year at Crozer, Dad had expanded his curriculum to include taking seven or eight of his students on a two-day seminar in New York, setting up interviews at the Interchurch Center and visiting a Commission on Colonial Affairs debate at the United Nations on British problems in Aden. His students were so enthusiastic about the experience that they wanted to make it a required course for the following year.[4]

## Vietnam Peace Efforts

Dad had no sooner returned from this trip when, the next morning while he was shaving, he received a phone call. A group of clergy concerned about Vietnam had been invited to meet with Secretary of Defense McNamara in Washington at 11:45 A.M., and Dad was asked to join the group:

> I got the fastest shave of my life, kissed Emilie good-bye, skipped breakfast, and followed a mess of traffic out to the airport—seven miles—just in time to get a cup of coffee and a donut and catch the 8:30 A.M. plane. On top of everything else, I was asked to be spokesman for the delegation, which I was reluctant to be, since I had missed the briefing session the night before.
>
> But I took it on, so had the responsibility of summarizing our position both to Mr. McNamara and to the press and TV people afterwards, with the result that I was on the Walter Cronkite program on TV that night. The points we made were:
>
> (1) an appeal for a cease-fire;
>
> (2) a more determined effort at a negotiated settlement;
>
> (3) a stepped-up program of economic development in the lower Mekong Valley;

(4) greater cooperation with the United Nations and less emphasis on unilateral action; and

(5) a clearer definition to the American public concerning our goals, whether limited to Vietnam or to some ultimate objective in Red China, with the possibility of a large-scale nuclear war.

We presented those points against the background of a thousand people who were standing around three sides of the Pentagon in a silent prayer vigil. Mr. McNamara gave us an excellent hearing, presented the government case strongly and effectively, and was most courteous in every way, at the same time that he pointed out both the areas of agreement and disagreement. He is one of the finest men we have ever had in government, and greatly admired by all for his factual presentations, his fluency of speech, and his pleasant manner. He had scheduled us for 30 minutes and kept us for 75, in what was a very forthright dialogue, around a table that was ringed with other tables covered with rifles, machine guns, bazookas, and all kinds of weaponry, plus flags, maps, and casualty charts day by day, week by week, and year by year.

Later I was taken over to the Senate Building by John Chambers of the United Press Radio for a ten-minute interview with Senator McGee of Wyoming, who is a very strong advocate of a hard-line policy—a case of "the hawks" vs. "the doves"—but who is a very fine and vigorous man to debate with. So it was a very rewarding day, and I notice that in tonight's paper there are many indications that what we argued for is being carried out, though only in part and maybe only temporarily. God alone knows the answers, but one of the great things about our form of government is that a group of citizens can come to the heads of government in this way.[5]

The following month, Dad went on a twelve-day fact-finding tour of Southeast Asia with a group of a dozen American men and women from the Fellowship of Reconciliation (FOR).[6] On his way to Saigon he passed through Bangkok, where he and I were able to meet briefly when I flew down from my hospital station in Mae Sariang, in northern Thailand, for a visit. I have to say that the research philosophy of some of his colleagues did not impress me as being up to Dad's own objective standards. I heard one of his "fact-seeking" colleagues excitedly report that, after an afternoon-long search, he had found a couple of Buddhist monks who agreed with the team's point of view. They did, however, contact many sources over the next week.

The group's interviewees in Bangkok included an official of the Thai Ministry of Education, who had some difficulty with English. The official turned the questions and answers over to a young Buddhist graduate of Yale and to an older man, the executive secretary of the Buddhist University, who oriented the group to Southeast Asian culture in general.

The men and women from FOR had lunch with U Kyaw Than of the East Asia Christian Council; he briefed them on relief work in Vietnam. Thereafter, they proceeded to the headquarters of SEATO (Southeast Asian Treaty Organization), where according to Dad's diary there was "little meeting of the minds," and to the U.S. Embassy, where they were told that there was no one with whom to negotiate in Vietnam (presumably meaning that there was no one in the Vietnam government having both the authority and the will to seek peaceful settlement).[7] The group then moved on to Saigon for interviews with Foreign Minister Tran Van Do, Buddhist leader Thich Tai Quang, the Catholic apostolic delegate for Vietnam, and various Catholic and Buddhist leaders, military and labor leaders, and embassy personnel. Areas of special interest for these interviews included agriculture, education, and health. FOR representatives found great differences of opinion among those whom they interviewed.

Dad took notes on the interviews as best he could, considering the large amount of information being given very quickly. The South Vietnamese foreign minister told the group that the United States had had nothing to do with starting the war. In 1954, the Geneva Agreement ended French colonialism in the area and divided Vietnam at the seventeenth parallel, prompting the migration of approximately one million Vietnamese from north to south, with few going from south to north. In 1960, there were 672 American "technicians" in Vietnam advising the South Vietnamese army on countermeasures against communist infiltration when the Vietcong guerrillas attacked.

Many American leaders hoped to create a social revolution in Vietnam. Yet President Lyndon Johnson's offer of $1 billion for economic aid in the Mekong area was greeted in Saigon with guffaws and jeers, and the Buddhists were as split as anyone else. Many of the Vietnam staff would like to see World War III, Dad noted in his diary. Someone asked what would happen if the present government should fall. "Contingency plans," came the answer. Vietcong prisoners were asked, "What would you do if we blew Hanoi off the map?" One replied, "Go back to the jungle and keep on fighting." The diary continues, "Every contact of Vietnamese peasant with government is [an] unpleasant one. Leaders are corrupt, and do nothing for [the] peasant."[8]

In a letter to the family, Dad wrote:

> The most exciting day of our stay in Saigon was the day we broke up into three or four groups for trips into the outlying countryside, where we could be away from Saigon officialdom. Two groups went down into the Mekong Delta

to see economic developments; one group went up to Cambodia; and five of us went to Song Be, some 70 miles north of Saigon where one of the bloodiest battles of the war was fought on May 12-13. We made the trip in a little Beechcraft plane, but flew at an altitude of 5,000 feet, fairly safe from Vietcong rifle fire. Song Be is at the edge of the central mountain area. The people there are very primitive, the men wearing loincloths.

Colonel Kanh and his American adviser, Major Sahey, gave us about the best picture of the situation that we got anywhere. Major Sahey is my idea of a top-notch army officer. He has only 46 American soldiers under him, all volunteers, but there are several hundred Vietnamese also. Sahey was in command the night of the battle, when 2,500 Vietcong attacked in force, and came near capturing the place. He described very vividly how the suicide squads would keep coming over the barbed wire barricades in groups of three, and how if one man was wounded or killed his two comrades would drag him away by means of the strap they all wear on their wrists, and how another group of three would come on in their place. The Vietcong were entrenched in the Catholic Church, directing such a deadly fire from the tower that he finally had to turn the guns on the church. They were repulsed after 24 hours with the help of American air strikes.

All the time Sahey was telling us this, mortar fire was blazing away only 150 yards from where we sat, and an air strike was going on six miles to our left. This was not an actual battle, but two Vietcong units were out in the jungle on the opposite side of the airport, and the mortar fire was to keep them pinned down. The whole place was being increasingly fortified, with foxholes, trenches, sandbags, barbed wire, and guns all over the place. A sad reminder of what is happening to the people was the fact that all the lovely young Vietnamese women waiting on table in the mess hall were already widows. We also saw hundreds of refugee children in a camp near by.[9]

On the group's arrival back in New York on July 11, they held a press conference, voicing their deep conviction of the need for an early cease-fire and peace negotiations: "The Vietnamese have been at war now for 25 years, and are so sick and weary of fighting that we are almost inevitably going to repeat the experience of the French if we stay on. There must of course be guarantees against a Communist takeover, but this can be accomplished if there is a determined effort to set up international controls to supervise the peace."[10] Dad's travel diary adds several notes:

The U.S. seems unable to distinguish between neutralism and Communism. In South Vietnam, people in war situation live in two worlds: as they would like it to be, and as it is. Impossible [for them] to be completely honest.

Can US and SVN win? French couldn't. U.S. could if it occupied all North and South with 500,000 U.S. troops—a new colonialism. China is not ready for world war, and Russia does not want it. Air raids will not win it, just create hatred. Vietnam people are the first victims, and suffer deeply on both sides. Two sets of facts have come to us, and we have to make value judgments. United Nations mediating body desirable, [but] limited by China's absence from, and U.S. by-passing, the U.N. Whatever the origins of the war, both sides are now trapped in it; war has become a way of life for both sides. The Vietcong can never win against the U.S., but can carry on war year after year far into the future. U.S. can win militarily, but only through actual attack on North Vietnam and prolonged occupation.

The fact-finding group from the Fellowship of Reconciliation offered these conclusions: "Emphasize responsibility to end war, and involve all other governments possible in this process. Encourage a belt of neutral nations."

Dad's diary adds, "The mistake of John Foster Dulles was turning political and national interests into a moral crusade. We blunder when we identify Washington policy as the Will of God."[11] The committee's published findings got them an invitation to Washington, where they held a two-hour conference with Secretary of Defense Robert McNamara, Secretary of State Dean Rusk, and Ambassador to the UN Arthur Goldberg.[12]

On 20 September 1965, the University of Michigan sponsored an interuniversity conference on foreign policy, with forty participants from twelve countries and all major religions. The last evening of the conference, Dad and the other participants fielded questions at a mass meeting attended by four thousand students, which overflowed into several smaller auditoriums and continued until about 2 A.M. Student speakers continued the dialogue outside until about 3:30.[13]

Soon after, the UN Association of Greater Phoenix invited Dad to speak at a protest meeting at the Arizona State University in Tempe in October. One thousand students and townspeople crowded the auditorium, with another eight hundred to a thousand outside who were unable to get in. The association later wrote him, "Your visit was the fuse that really set things in action."[14]

## The *Crusader* Debate

It should be noted that some people at the time reacted favorably to advice from the clergy about foreign policy and Vietnam; some of these were national leaders, such as Robert McNamara, who, in retrospect thirty years later, has admitted questioning the wisdom of the U.S.

involvement in Vietnam. On the other hand, there were many at the time, including many Christians, who saw U.S. intervention as a necessary act.

In December 1965, five months after the Fellowship of Reconciliation team had publicized its proposals, Dad entered into a written discussion of Vietnam with *Crusader* editor Paul C. Allen. Allen disagreed with the FOR and posed five questions, each preceded by informational background material.[15] Both questions and replies appeared in the February 1966 issue and are condensed to some degree here.

In introducing a background for the discussion, Allen quoted Soviet Premier Aleksei Kosygin: "We believe that 'wars of national liberation' are just wars, and they will continue as long as there is national oppression by imperialist powers. . . . In South Viet Nam there is a national liberation war."[16]

Allen quoted similar declarations by several other communist leaders and then commented, "In summary, it would seem that (1) while proclaiming peace, the communists have reserved for themselves a special device for waging wars of their own choosing; (2) that such wars are moral while American counteraction is immoral . . . some means must be found for countering them or innumerable 'imperialist' countries around the world will fall prey to such tactics."

Against this backdrop, Allen posed the following question: "How would you propose to deal with 'wars of national liberation' as they are launched by communists around the world?"

Dad replied that American policy is often defective in supporting dictatorial regimes like those of Batista in Cuba and Ngo Dinh Diem and Madame Nu in Saigon, thus affording communists the initiative in freeing the villagers from predatory landlordism. Dad indicated that he favored multinational action, rather than unilateral action by the U.S., and stressed the need to turn away from military force, which destroyed piecemeal the small nation it purported to save, and to turn more toward economic and political solutions.

Allen's next question focused on multinational action: "What multinational or multi-lateral force (other than the U.S. and allies now serving with it) could realistically be expected to move into Viet Nam if the U.S. should either withdraw or be immobilized? Without such a force, is not the course of self-determination hopelessly lost?"

We had already doomed the cause of self-determination, replied Dad, by blocking the free elections promised to Vietnam in 1954 by the Geneva Agreement. He acknowledged that we cannot withdraw abruptly from

Vietnam, leaving a vacuum. "The United Nations has admittedly been weakened, partly because we bypassed it in Vietnam and partly because of Soviet Russia's refusal to pay its membership dues and financial obligations involved in the Congo operations." But, in the words of a British journalist, "We do not smash the Stradivarius just because the violinist played it badly." The United Nations and the nations of Southeast Asia, including North and South Vietnam and even the Vietcong and Red China, would all have to be involved, or there could be no solution. In Dad's estimation, "This will be tough, in view of the fact that all the nations fear each other and hate each other. But it will be no tougher than the continuation of this bloody, brutal war."

The third question posed by Allen alluded to the so-called domino theory: "If an effective counter-deterrent of some sort is not maintained in Southeast Asia, will not Thailand, Malaysia, surely Burma and probably India go down the communist drain by force, intimidation or insurgency? Are you willing to gamble on a deterrent not now in sight (other than U.S. force) to prevent this? Then what about the Philippines? If the U.S. should stand firm somewhere, where is that 'somewhere'?" Dad acknowledged that some nations could fall if Vietnam fell, but that it did not necessarily need to happen. The process stopped in Europe. Most nations there did not go communist, and of those that did, some—Yugoslavia, for example—put their own nationalism above the world-conquering, messianic ambitions of the type of communism in Red China.

Next Allen posed a question about stopping the bombing of North Vietnam: "What assurance do we have that if we stop the bombing, the Communists will not use this hiatus to regroup, re-supply, re-enforce and generally strengthen their position?" Dad agreed that the Vietcong would probably do this. He pointed out, however, that they were already doing this despite the bombing—the Ho Chi Minh trail was protected by dense foliage that the U.S. bombs so far had been unable to penetrate effectively. But more important, the bombing served only to harden the resistance of the Vietnamese people and to damage the U.S. reputation. We may temporarily "lose face" by pulling out, as did the French a decade before, but we shall also lose it if we continue to bomb and be bled white in the process.

Allen's final question focused on demonstrations at home: "While the right to protest is inviolable in the democratic system, do the demonstrators who march on Washington (and do other similar things) ever consider the wisdom of it? Is it not true that in thus encouraging the enemy they may be increasing his will to resist, thus raising the toll of both American and Vietnamese lost in battle—the exact opposite of what they are trying to achieve. If they do consider these things, how do they reconcile them?" Dad began his reply by considering the demonstrators:

> The American public should know that some of the most responsible elements in our national life have been involved in the protest movements. . . . Among them were many members of the American Legion wearing their battle stars, middle-aged fathers and mothers, preachers, priests, and rabbis. They were there to do what Congress has never [yet] done: debate the moral issues of this inhuman war. . . .
>
> The question was a proper one: do not such demonstrations increase the will of the enemy to resist, thus raising the number of Americans and Vietnamese killed in battle? Put in another way, as some ask, "Are you not betraying our men who are bleeding and dying in the jungles and rice fields of Viet Nam—stabbing them in the back, as it were?"
>
> Not at all. Is it betrayal of the more than 1,000 young Americans who have already died and the more than 5,000 who have been wounded if we seek to protect thousands more of our best American youth from having to suffer the same fate? It is time to say with all the patriotic and religious conviction of our souls, "In the name of God, stop it!"
>
> As far as hardening the resistance of the enemy is concerned, all the protesters from Washington to California will not encourage the enemy as much as the dropping of one napalm bomb on the villages and rice fields of Viet Nam.

United Nations General Secretary U Thant and Pope Paul VI had appealed to all belligerents to end the war, noted Dad. He then continued, "Must those who are Protestant Christians always be charged with subversion, treason, and betrayal if, in the name of Christ and all that is best in our American tradition, we too make the same plea?" He then concluded with these words:

> I am perfectly aware that I am no political or military expert. But I have been within 150 yards of the firing line. I have seen the widows and the refugee children and the old people of South Viet Nam; the bombed-out churches . . . the tired, war-weary villagers. . . . As a minister of the gospel of Jesus Christ, having seen these things, I think I could ask some questions even more difficult to answer than those submitted to me:
>
> What is happening to the character of man? . . . What is going to be the answer even if we do win a military victory? How are we going to win the peace? And how many billions of dollars in additional taxes will it cost, to say nothing of the American homes plunged into sorrow? . . . How are we going to answer to Jesus Christ, of whom the Apostle Paul said that he came 'to bring

the hostility to an end,' and to 'preach peace to those who are far off and to those who are near.' (Eph 2:14-18) If the cross of Calvary is going to mean anything to our time, we had better begin preaching it as something more than a doctrine and be prepared to demonstrate it as an experience. . . .

Editor Allen wrapped up the discussion:

> We would like to challenge Dr. Dahlberg's reasoning and conclusions at several places in the above text, but we refrain from doing so in the interest of "the rules of the game." After all, editors should not always be privileged to have the last word. . . . Whether Dr. Dahlberg's responses meet the challenge of these questions will be for each reader to decide. But of the honesty, concern and Christian intent of both points of view there can be no question. *Crusader* invites response from its constituency in the same spirit in which these questions were asked and answered.

Response from readers, published in the April 1966 issue, was divided.[17] Two letters are fairly representative: that of Rev. Robert Olson of Linwood, N.J., and James H. Mowe of Denver. Olson disagreed with Dad, saying, ". . . Dr. Dahlberg speaks of the responsibility of the church to speak out. Obviously it is to speak out for peace. But does not the church also have a concern for justice? Should the church condone compromise with evil? . . . Does taking the way of the cross mean we publicly advocate surrender to communism? I know of no instance in the scripture where Christ compromised himself or his word, or suggests that we should." Mowe sided with Dad, writing,

> . . . It is my opinion that history will vindicate Dr. Dahlberg and the other critics of the present U.S. policy in Viet Nam.
>
> It is a cruel, bloody war and there is blame on both sides. The present administration seems determined to continue in our present course despite the grave risks involved and mounting dissatisfaction in our own country. It is possible that victory can be achieved ultimately at great human and material cost through the application of massive military power, but what will be gained in the long run if, in the process, we destroy the country whose freedom we are fighting to protect?
>
> . . . I prefer to be in favor of the dove-like, reconciling approach of Dr. Dahlberg . . . than to be in favor of the opposing hard-line approach which you support.

Allen replied in a personal letter to Mowe:

> Dear friend Mowe: Thank you for your note regarding Dr. Dahlberg, etc. Ed Dahlberg and I have known each other for some time. I consider him a fine and sincere Christian leader, even though I differ with him considerably as to how we can best achieve peace in our time and our world. We must never lose

sight of the fact that both of us are primarily interested in peace, and that the only difference between us is how best to achieve peace.

Someday when I am long since gone from this post, I hope I will be remembered as an editor who had his own strong convictions, but who tried to be fair to other responsible Christians in their own points of view. I consider what we have printed together is a demonstration of this.[18]

Dad recognized that there were people of integrity on both sides of the debate. His own uncompromising stand for peaceful negotiation was not blind optimism, but a conviction that settlement by force of arms inevitably escalated into disastrous and largely unnecessary destruction and loss of life. He saw a strong desire in the United States for a negotiated settlement, if it could be brought about without surrendering Southeast Asia to communism.[19] He believed that the United Nations was becoming little more than a debating society, like the old League of Nations, and thought that many opportunities for peace were being lost there.[20]

## Peace March on Washington

Dad was resolved that the alternative of peace must be kept before the public eye despite the angry charges that flew from those who believed that there could be no negotiation. He therefore participated in peaceful confrontation and joined in some of the peace marches in Washington, D.C. On the night of 13 November 1969, at the age of seventy-seven, he was one of forty thousand who marched silently, twenty feet apart in single file, each bearing a candle and a placard with the name of someone who had died in the Vietnam conflict. They marched past the White House, each pausing at the gate to call out the name of the deceased soldier whose name the placard bore, and on to the Capitol to deposit the name in one of several white caskets as drummers with muffled drums beat a solemn funeral roll. The procession took from 6 P.M. Thursday until 10 A.M. Saturday to pass—one thousand names per hour, or one name about every four seconds for forty hours—the marchers pausing only for traffic lights, where marshals from the group guided them across each intersection as the light turned green.

Dad, who was in one of the first contingents, wrote to us of the experience:

I thought it was significant that during the entire three hours I was marching I did not hear a single jeer or catcall, nor was there any heckling, such as we usually encounter. There was a feeling of reverence all along the line.

The man in charge of all the peace marshals was a Marine lieutenant who had declined a captaincy and chose to become a conscientious objector instead, having come to the conclusion that this particular war is senseless and wrong. I was impressed by the number of war veterans in the march, as well as by the number of families of the dead. Both the military and the police were most friendly and cooperative.

Unfortunately, the demonstration was marred Friday night by one of the radical revolutionary groups such as the Students for a Democratic Society, the Crazy Cats, and the Wild Dogs, whose actions the Moratorium Committee vigorously repudiated. These violent nuts always give the demonstrations a black eye, by throwing rocks and bottles and breaking windows, taunting the police until the latter let go with tear gas.

Friday, yesterday, I attended a breakfast of the Baptist Peace Fellowship in the morning, and a workshop of the Fellowship of Reconciliation during the day. Last night there was a dinner with 250 invited guests, each paying eight dollars, but which consisted only of a cup of tea and a bowl of rice, the surplus funds going to the Committee of Responsibility, which is bringing terribly burned and wounded Vietnamese children to the United States for surgery and rehabilitation.

I hope the huge mass demonstration today can be an orderly one. The marchers were already gathering by the thousands as I was on the way to the airport at 7:30 this morning.[21]

In 1971, continuing to hold to his vision of world peace, Dad made an uncharacteristic gesture of passive resistance by deliberately withholding a part of his federal income tax. In a letter to the Internal Revenue Service on April 5, he stated:

I do not wish to evade my duties as a loyal American citizen. I love my country, and will do anything I can to serve it honorably. But I cannot in good conscience continue to contribute my tax dollars to the slaughter in Laos, Cambodia, and Vietnam. . . . For more than fifty years I have employed every lawful procedure I could think of to bring this procession of death to an end: by voting, demonstrating, petitioning, writing, preaching, praying. Apparently it has all been in vain. As an adult citizen beyond draft age, I can now think of no other way to make my protest than by withholding some proportion of my income tax that would otherwise go for military purposes.[22]

Dad withheld $100 of the $227 that was due and donated it to poverty groups and peace organizations in the Phoenix area. The IRS sent him formal notice that his action was illegal but did not pursue the matter, perhaps not wishing to make a public issue in this case.

Protest works both ways. In 1973, the Dahlberg Peace Award nominee was Dr. William Sloane Coffin Jr., who had a very high profile among the

protesters of the Vietnam War at that time. The General Board of the
American Baptists contained a wide spectrum of attitudes toward
Vietnam in those days, some more hawkish than others. Some raised a
proposal that the Dahlberg Peace Award be withheld that year, rather than
award it to Coffin. Dr. Paul Lewis recalls the controversy at the American
Baptist Convention in Lincoln, Nebraska:

> As I entered [the convention center], a man came up to me and wanted me
> to sign a petition objecting to William Sloane Coffin Jr. being given the
> Dahlberg Peace Prize. I said that I highly respected him and thought it was a
> good choice, but the man said, "Well, Dr. Dahlberg's widow feels it is a terri-
> ble mistake, and we think that Dr. Dahlberg would object as well if he were
> still alive." I told them that Mrs. Dahlberg had passed away, but that Dr.
> Dahlberg was in a nearby hotel at that moment. I don't think he really believed
> me, but I went to your Dad and asked if he could come with me to the con-
> vention center. . . . I introduced him to the man who had asked me to sign the
> petition. "This is Dr. Dahlberg, maybe you could ask him about the peace
> prize," I said.
>
> Well, your Dad went into action shaking hands with the several individuals
> who were collecting signatures. He explained to them that he really had noth-
> ing to do with the selection; that was done by a committee. It was named for
> him because he was so concerned about peace. "As far as I know, every per-
> son they have chosen is first rate," he said, "and I certainly couldn't agree more
> on William Sloane Coffin Jr." Then he began to ask them their names and
> where they lived. Right away he recognized the first man and began talking to
> him about his father, and working with him in the past. It was great to see your
> Dad "in action."[23]

Dad played no part in these peace award nominations, but this time he
intervened. "If the peace award should be withdrawn," he wrote, "are we
not then following the example of the Soviet Union, which has on several
occasions withdrawn peace awards and literary awards from its most distinguished writers because these awards have incurred the displeasure of
the government authorities? I would hope that we would all take to heart
what Dr. Coffin is trying to teach us: the truth of Christ as expressed in
Romans 12:17-21."[24] The motion to withdraw the award failed, in any
case, and Coffin received the award. The matter became moot as the
Vietnam War passed into history.

# Chapter 10

# Pastor Emeritus

*Successful retirement is not mere cessation of work; rather, it is working at something satisfying, at one's own pace and on one's own schedule. Edwin T. Dahlberg found a number of churches in temporary need of his services and traveled extensively.*

In July of 1965, Dad and Mother left Crozer. The school had wanted them to stay on another year, but Dad wanted to give more time to writing, and both had reached an age where the winters were stressful. They entered Orangewood, a Baptist-administered retirement community in Phoenix, Arizona, and joined the First Baptist Church of Phoenix nearby.

Retired clergy often serve short periods at churches in need of an interim pastor. Over the next decade or more, Dad was a supply pastor to several churches across the nation, including the little one that my family and I attend in Osburn, Idaho. It is a win/win situation; the church gets the benefit of experienced clergy who can apply their talents to whatever local problems exist. The temporary pastor has salary needs less than that of a younger pastor with a growing family, giving the church time to get back on its feet financially in many cases. The pastor gets the fulfillment of being back at work for a few months without the long-term responsibility, which will be taken over shortly by a new pastor. Being a supply minister is sort of like being a grandparent—enjoy the baby but hand it back to the parents before it cries. But even interim pastors sometimes encounter crises.

"I'm going to jump in the river!" The young woman who had been slumped down in her chair in Dad's office suddenly jumped up and headed for the door. She had come in late one afternoon in suicidal despair, one of the victims of a previous minister's sexual misconduct within his flock. Dad could tell she really meant it and followed her, but she was walking so fast, going in and out of the busy 5 P.M. traffic that it was all he could do to keep her in sight. When he finally caught up with her, he did not know what passersby thought was going on as she clutched a parking meter and kept saying, "Nobody cares for me! I can't live in this hell anymore. There's no God. No use your praying anymore. Let me go!"

"Nobody cares?" said Dad. "Well, at least I care. Do you suppose I would have followed you through all this crowd if I didn't care?" This seemed to strike home; she went back to the church with him, and a doctor admitted her to a psychiatric ward until she was out of danger.

Repairing damage done by the sexual misconduct of previous clergy was one of the most difficult problems with which Dad had to deal in churches where he was an interim pastor. It shatters a congregation, causing bitter recriminations, broken homes, division between those who recognize the evidence and those still in denial, and even spawning lawsuits, which can bankrupt a church community. Some people are irretrievably lost, never again willing to trust those who call themselves Christian. Dad wrote about his approach to one situation in which such misconduct had occurred: "If I am to make any headway with [the ex-pastor] at all I feel I must both be brutally frank, and also appeal to . . . his Christian faith and the personal fellowship we have had in the ministry. . . . Obviously he is a sick man, physically, mentally, and spiritually. For healing he would probably need the three-fold ministry of a doctor, psychiatrist, and a skilled pastoral counsellor . . . it may be necessary to expose him, without revealing the names of the women concerned." The former pastor refused to admit wrongdoing, but evidence mounted up—written statements from women the man had seduced and reports by others of his obscene phone calls.[1]

Dad mused, "What ever happened to sin? . . . In what some theologians call 'the new paganism,' God is only a memory of something they remembered their grandparents believed, or else [they] have been sold on the idea that God is dead." By the time Dad finished his interim, he had managed to bring a degree of healing to the congregation and to some individuals, but the former pastor's irresponsibility left long-term damage. Dad quoted a word of advice to those who had forgotten their calling, "It is extremely difficult to be godly without God."

During the late 1960s, it seemed that Mother and Dad had finally retired. Dad would have continued to travel, but Mother's health began to deteriorate, and they stayed at home more and more. They still carried on an enormous correspondence with friends, former church members, and various church groups; they sent six hundred Christmas cards each year and received at least that many. They had more time for evening reading or testing each other at Scrabble or even watching TV, which they had almost never done before.

Mother had long had arthritis in her back and was developing heart failure as well. In late 1967, the muscle spasms and breathlessness ended her ability to travel at all, and Dad canceled most of his speaking appointments to be with her. By the summer of 1968, she had been in the hospital several times and was confined to a chair, sometimes barely able to communicate through the haze of medication. On other days she was well enough to go to the hairdresser in a wheelchair or to bake cookies. On July 13, she complimented Dad on the supper he had prepared for her and then later that evening died quite suddenly. Although he pressed the emergency bell (with which every apartment was equipped), there was nothing the resident nurse could do when she arrived moments later.

It was one month before their golden wedding anniversary.

Dad was well acquainted with the sorrow of death, but it strikes again each time someone is lost. There are no words that really help at such a time. My sister, Margaret, and I flew to Phoenix; Bruce was in Jordan at the time and arrived later. Accompanied on the piano by Margaret, cousin Marjorie sang "Come Ye Disconsolate," an old hymn that ends, "Earth has no sorrow that Heaven cannot heal." Dr. L. Doward McBain, Mother and Dad's pastor in Phoenix and an old friend, led the memorial service.

Dad did his grieving, supported by family and friends, and then continued with his life. Freed of the need to stay close to Orangewood, he began to travel again. He racked up some twelve thousand miles on his car's odometer each summer over the next few years, as he traveled to temporary pastorates across the continent. He interspersed these with conventions and seminars and vacation time.

He recorded a four-and-a-half-pound northern pike caught in a Minnesota lake, and he struck up an acquaintance with the family that then owned the old family farm in Fergus Falls. He went back to check out the farm each summer, thinking each year might be his last opportunity, and thus he came to know them quite well. As do many senior citizens, he took increasing interest in history, and many of his trips were to help celebrate anniversaries—the 270th of Philadelphia's First Baptist Church, the 150th of his own first church in Potsdam, New York, the 30th of the American Baptist Assembly Grounds in Green Lake, Wisconsin, his 60th reunion of the class of 1914 at the University of Minnesota. (The president of the university introduced the 1914 class to the present undergraduates as the last class that had known peace throughout the world.)

Dad continued to be active in the Baptist Peace Fellowship, of which he was a charter member, and the Fellowship of Reconciliation, which he had joined in 1920, five years after it was formed. Reconciliation sometimes included confrontation. Richard Deats, a longtime member of the FOR, recalls a conference at the Green Lake assembly grounds when FOR members were supporting the United Farm Workers. When several members discovered that the cafeteria was serving nonunion lettuce, they created a near riot in the dining room, throwing salad on the floor and making strong protest to the cafeteria supervisor. The supervisor countered that the food was supplied by a Chicago-based service and that local staff had no say in where lettuce came from. At that point, Dad stepped in to calm the protesters and join their meeting with the food staff and conference management. Deats credits him with persuading the management to tell Chicago that no more nonunion lettuce would be accepted. He observes that it was a happy coincidence that Dr. Dahlberg was not only an FOR member but chairman of the assembly grounds' fund-raising drive that year.[2]

Dad had more time to enjoy visits with his children and grandchildren, who were afforded the opportunity to hear some of the stories in their grandfather's immense fund. He would accompany us on vacations to the Oregon coast and once to San Francisco, but was still independent. Coming back from Oregon, he once left us at Ellensburg, Washington, to catch a northbound bus for Wenatchee to visit an old high-school friend he had not seen in many years.

In Orangewood, Dad was one of four ministers in residence to the two hundred or so senior citizens who were his neighbors. He knew most of them by this time, having met them in the dining room or on the walkways, and was able to be a very real help to one or another on occasion. He still delighted in making new friends, as is evident from an encounter he described in a Christmas letter: "I was walking past a parked car on my way into a store when a four-year-old little girl called to me from the open window of the car, 'What's your name?' On the spur of the moment I said, 'My name is Grandpa. What's your name, honey?'

"'My name is Lisa,' she replied, and then added brightly, 'How old are you?'

"'I am eighty-three. And how old are you, Lisa?'

"Evidently quite impressed, she stammered, 'I'm—I'm—89!' Then it was my turn to be impressed.

"That ended the conversation. Except that when I had completed my errand, she waved to me all the way back to my car, calling out 'Goodbye,

Grandpa!' I shall probably never meet Lisa again on this earth. But that brief exchange made my day."[3]

## Viola

At the end of 1976, after years of solo travel, Dad wrote his children that in a week or two he would have an important announcement to make. The "Watch This Space!" format was so uncharacteristic of him that I told my wife facetiously, "Either Dad is about to get a new car or a new wife!" Lois and I had occasionally speculated about Dad and matrimony. In the nine years since Mother had died, we had detected a slightly proprietary attitude on the part of several ladies in and around Orangewood. But the announcement, in his New Year's letter of 1977, introduced someone entirely new.[4]

Viola Palmiter, a trim, vivacious, sixty-seven-year-old widow, had only recently moved to Orangewood, after returning from two years teaching English in a girls' school in Japan. The previous summer, she had been on the summer staff at the American Baptist Assembly in Green Lake, Wisconsin, when Dad had led a week's series of vesper services there. Though each knew who the other was, they had not met till one afternoon in Phoenix when Viola was returning from the grocery store and paused at the corner of 14th and Belmont to get her bearings. Dad came around the corner in his car and offered her a lift. "No, thank you. My mother told me never to accept rides from strangers," answered the lady, demurely. "I don't know why that came out," she told me years later. "I just was out for a walk, I guess. I asked him to just point my feet in the right direction, and he did." "If I hadn't," Dad reportedly observed later, "she'd have ended up at the Grand Canyon, the way she was headed."

The relationship moved swiftly thereafter. A mutual friend told Viola there was no reason why she could not ride along to church with them in "Dr. D's" car, and it was only a month or so later when Dad proposed to her on his eighty-fourth birthday, and she accepted. In the New Year's Day letter to the family, Dad said,

> In all the years since your mother left us, thoughts of further romance have never entered my mind. For one thing, I wanted to be loyal to her memory, as well as be fair to you children. Still further, I had seen so many old men make fools of themselves by marrying someone who was maybe fifty years younger than they were that I thought it would be silly for me to even entertain such a thought. I couldn't help thinking of the two old gaffers sitting on one of the

street benches down in St. Petersburg, Florida, talking one Sunday night about their hometowns up north. "How did you happen to come down here to Florida?" one of them asked the other. "Well, my wife died, and it was pretty lonely around the old place after that. So I thought I would come down here and maybe find me another wife." "That's why I came," said the man who had raised the question, "I wish to God you had got here first!"

I didn't want to get caught in that trap, so I stayed single. But it really is pretty lonely to stay single. After sitting alone in your apartment night after night, watching TV or reading a magazine, you long for some understanding person who would be fun to talk to, and who would provide the affection and companionship that you have missed since the one you loved was gone. To come to the point, I have discovered that person . . . [and he went on to describe her]. I wrote a chapter in a book way back in 1934 on "Problems of Second Marriage."[5] Little did I realize that forty years later I would be reading it again while seeking some counsel for myself!

One of his friends, Dr. Carlyle Marney, when told of Dad's plans by a mutual friend, dropped the fork he held and exclaimed "He *what?* Why he's old enough to know better!"[6] Nevertheless, Dad had indeed found the right person. We didn't meet her until the wedding on February 17 (courtships at age eighty-four are not protracted). "She is very attractive, both in personality and appearance," I wrote to those unable to attend, "almost as tall as Dad, poised, pleasant, and appears to enjoy life. She and Dad are very attentive to each other. We all think he made a very good choice."

The wedding itself was memorable. One of the pictures that stands out in my mind is of a blazing gold-and-pink Arizona sunset filling the sky and reflecting on the mountains, as I watched Dad stride briskly away to the chapel to meet his bride. The chapel, which seats maybe 150, was full. There was an organ and piano prelude, and then with very little fanfare Dad and Viola walked down the aisle together without attendants, but preceded by the minister, Dr. Charles Carman. Dad wore a white suit with blue shirt and black bow tie. Viola was beautifully dressed in a handmade long-sleeved gown of pink silk from India trimmed with gold and carried a small bouquet. The wedding vows were traditional in style, spoken very clearly and confidently. Dad muffed one line, like any first-time groom, and the minister dropped the ring, but otherwise the ceremony went smoothly. At the close, a procession formed spontaneously outside the chapel, with Dad and Viola walking hand in hand with Dr. Carman down the covered walkway to the reception, followed at a distance by her family, then ours, and then the others in the audience.

The reception featured the usual wedding cake, photographs, little speeches, and a few songs and other performances thrown in. One of Dad's cronies from Minnesota, a Mr. Bloom, gave a very straight-faced speech in Swedish dialect, explaining that Dad had originally volunteered to participate in an energy-saving plan to share his apartment with some other Orangewood resident, but when he drew a name out of the hat, "it vasn't Charlie at all, but somebody named Wi-o-la." The romance, as told by Bloom, then proceeded through various stages: window shopping ("That's a beautiful wedding suit in the window!" "That's not a wedding suit; that's a business suit." "Well, I mean business."), sending out wedding invitations ("RSVP, dot stands for Remember Send Vedding Presents"), and aspects of the premarital medical exam, which surprised Dad's teenage and adult grandchildren but did not seem to bother the wheel-chaired audience. My son, John, was most taken with the line that Grandpa has special influence in heaven because when a Swede prays, "God don't have to translate."[7]

The bride and groom honeymooned briefly in Tucson.

Now that Dad once more had a traveling companion, he roamed the world with new enthusiasm. Dad and Viola spent several months at a time in interim pastorates, attended conferences and conventions, even visited us at the mission hospital in Thailand.[8]

Dad also took renewed interest in writing. He had authored one book in 1934, *Youth in the Homes of Tomorrow,* and had edited another,[9] contributing a chapter of his own. He also had written many pamphlets over the years. The folders of poetry in his files are mostly poems sent him by various church members. I have discovered only one authored by him: "Psalm of the Sugarbush"—in whimsical praise of maple syrup.[10] Several other book-length works had faltered before reaching publication, perhaps partly because of the cryptic titles he chose—*The Bullwheel,* for instance, or *By the Waters of Meribah.* Several chapters of an unfinished autobiography lie in his "sermon barrel."

In 1978, however, he chose a straightforward title and subject with which readers could empathize, *I Pick Up Hitchhikers.*[11] During his years as a widower, driving twelve to fifteen thousand miles a year, curiosity and sympathy had led him to pick up many people who were thumbing their way along the nation's highways. "I realized it could be dangerous," he acknowledged, "but if an eighty-year-old gets hit on the head, it's not the tragedy it would be in a younger person's life." He met an amazing variety of people this way. Dad began each chapter with a few of their anecdotes and then went on to supply a bit of his own philosophy of life and faith in God. He didn't try to high-pressure any of his passengers but made a quiet observation to each on something relevant to what he heard the hitchhiker say. Occasionally he bought one a meal, but usually he just gave a lift down the road. Sometimes he got a letter from one later. When he remarried, he stopped the practice because he was unwilling to submit Viola to the same risks he would take for himself.

Dad's speaking career continued. Though he was approaching the age of ninety, he was fond of announcing that his doctor declared him "strong as an ox!" In 1982, Dad and Viola both served on the summer staff at the American Baptist Assembly in Green Lake—he as chaplain, she as a hostess. In the fall, they attended a 325-member conference on world peace in Washington D.C., and Dad was interviewed by one of the conference leaders. A news media assistant recalls his own consternation at seeing this old man wandering about among the TV cables backstage: "I was terrified he would trip and have a major injury. But as we were going offstage, down the steps, it was I who tripped, and Dr. Dahlberg who reached out a hand to steady me!"

At the age of ninety, when Dad and Viola were in Europe, he was invited to Moscow to preach in the one Baptist church the Soviet government permitted to stay open. (Next to the Russian Orthodox Church, Baptists were possibly the largest Christian group in the Soviet Union at that time.) He preached the gospel of Jesus Christ to a standing-room-only crowd of two thousand in the heart of the Communist empire as his last public achievement. From 1983 onward, although he visited, and was visited by, many friends and family and continued some correspondence, he was retired from public life.

# Chapter 11

# Family

*The story of Edwin T. Dahlberg is not defined simply by his service in the church and in the cause of peace. He was also son, brother, husband, father, uncle, grandfather, friend.*

Despite his perennially heavy schedule of church pastoring, committee meetings, and travel, Dad took time for his family. When we were little children, Saturday evenings were always for family, never for committees. He and Mother both would take time to read to us. No matter if we insisted on starting each time "at the beginning!" they were patient. Either parent could probably have recited the first chapter of the *Wizard of Oz* from memory.

On the Fourth of July, Dad helped us set off firecrackers and made sure that we did not blow a finger off with a cherry bomb. Each Thanksgiving, he led us children, and any visiting cousins, on a predinner hike across the hills. Soon after Easter one year when we were small, Dad stopped the car at a wooded area and suggested we might possibly find the Easter bunny's hole in the woods and leave a thank-you note for all the Easter baskets we had found hidden around our house the night before Easter. We did indeed find a hole at the base of one tree, wrote the note, signed it, and put it deep in the hole. Several days later, while out driving, Dad suggested we find out if the bunny had left an answer. Sure enough, we found a reply, written on birch bark, deep in the hole! Mystery—how had it gotten there?

"Easter bunnies, chocolate eggs, and jelly beans are of course only the pagan side of Easter," Dad wrote years later, "but who shall say that children and parents do not get a lot of fun out of these traditions, and even some enrichment for their Christian family life? Provided—that we keep alive the true gospel story of Easter: the crucifixion, the resurrection, and the good news of Christ's rising from the dead."[1]

Nils and Johanna Danielson Dahlberg, Edwin's grandparents, who emigrated from Sweden in 1870.

Edwin's parents, Elof and Christina, at the time of their engagement, 1879.

Edwin's family circa 1901. Back row (left to right): Effie, Arnold, Henry, Irene. Seated: father Elof, Edwin, mother Christina.

Delivering newspapers for the *Minneapolis Tribune* circa 1908. Edwin built up his route to 175 customers.

Edwin T. Dahlberg, circa 1918.

Mother on her wedding day, 1918.

Rutledge Wiltbank, the Minneapolis pastor who encouraged Dad to enter the ministry.

Walter Rauschenbusch, Dad's professor and mentor in seminary.
[Photo from the American Baptist Historical Society]

Our family circa 1938. Left to right:
Margaret, Mother, Keith, Dad, Bruce.

Maple St. Baptist Church,
Buffalo, New York, circa 1924.

Dad nears the top of Longo
Peak in Colorado, 1943.
[Photo by Bruce Dahlberg]

First Baptist Church, Syracuse, New
York, circa 1940.
[Photo from the church's 125th Anniversary Book]

At Green Lake, Wisconsin (left to right): Dad, Mother, C. Oscar Johnson, Mrs. Johnson, Janet Dahlberg, Bruce Dahlberg, circa 1952.

Syracuse First Baptist Church staff circa 1945. Standing (left to right): Alfred Scipione, Assistant Pastor; Edwin T. Dahlberg, Pastor; John T. Clough, Minister of Music. Seated (left to right): George Oplinger, Organist; Mrs. Wm. A. Sanderson, Secretary; Mrs. John T. Clough, Minister of Music; Warren L. Adams, Minister of Christian Education.
[Photo from the church's 125th Anniversary Book]

Margaret, Mother, Dad, with granddaughters Gail and Joan, circa 1953.

During Alaska Christmas tour, 1957, Kodiak Baptist Mission Home children gave Dad a party on his 65th birthday.
[Photo from the Office of the General Secretary, ABC/USA]

Kodiak, Alaska, Dr. Dahlberg reviews a Marine honor guard on his Christmas tour of Alaska, 1957.
[Photo from the American Baptist Historical Society]

Dad addresses a celebration of Israel's 10th national anniversary, New York, 1958.
[Photo from the American Baptist Historical Society]

Dad and President Eisenhower greet well-wishers at the cornerstone-laying ceremony for the Interchurch Center building, New York, 1958. [Photo from the American Baptist Historical Society]

Dad presides and J. Irwin Miller speaks from the podium on the unemployment statement adopted by the National Council of Churches Board, 1958. (Photo from NCC/Audio-Visual Service)

Visiting with Airman Billy Matkins at Sidi Salmane Airbase, Morocco, on Christmas tour of Spain and North Africa, 1958.
[Photo from the American Baptist Historical Society]

Delivering "The Churches and the National Conscience" address at Hartford, Connecticut, 1959.
[Photo from NCC/George Conklin]

Supreme Patriarch Vasken I. (on Dad's left), of the Ancient Church of Armenia, presents a tablet, 1960. [Photo from NCC]

Dad and Mother, 1962, at the time of their retirement.

Three presidents of the National Council of Churches (left to right): Dad (1958 through 1960), J. Irwin Miller (1961 through 1963), Eugene Carson Blake (1955 through 1957), at the NCC General Assembly meeting in San Francisco in December 1960.
[Photo from NCC/Milton Mann Studios]

Dad conferring with Thra Tun Shein, secretary of the Burma Baptist Convention.
[Photo from the Office of the General Secretary, ABC/USA]

Viola and Dad, circa 1977.

First Dahlberg Peace Award presentation, 1964. First row (left to right): Martin Luther King Jr., Mrs. King, Dad, Mrs. and Mr. Victor Gavel (sponsors of the award), Senator Hubert Humphrey. At the podium, former Minnesota Governor Harold Stassen.

In all my childhood, I do not recall any teaching about Satanism in Halloween or the pagan origins of Christmas trees and gifts. We had no disillusionment with God on being told by friends that there was no Santa Claus; we understood that there was a difference. We were given to understand that God is more powerful than any powers of darkness and that with faith and a little common sense, we need have no fear of them. Actually, Dad could carve a pretty good pumpkin, and he, in turn, was properly impressed with my teenage chemistry skill of making green Halloween fire from boric acid and alcohol.

Vacation time was always the high point of the year. The whole family would pile into the car (in our preteen years, at least), three children strategically separated to prevent warfare, and we would head for the Lake Erie shore at Kingsville, Ontario, or better yet for Colorado, where all the rest of the Dahlberg clan had settled by then and where Uncle Henry had a cabin up in the gold-mining town of Ward. There might be twenty of us cousins, aunts, and uncles gathered around the table for pancakes or around a campfire or exploring mine dumps for fool's gold. Or there would be clan picnics in one of the Denver parks or a trip to see the wonders around Colorado Springs. The only other event whose attraction even approached Colorado reunions was Dad's taking us to the state fair, with its rides, sideshows, cattle exhibits, and, at the evening's finale, a burst of fireworks in the sky!

We children had friends in school and around the neighborhood, but it's as natural for preachers' kids to grow up around the church as it is for country kids to be familiar with the farm. Margaret, Bruce, and I are spaced about five years apart so that, although we shared part of childhood, we each traveled with a different crowd. Much of our social life related to the Baptist Youth Fellowship (or Baptist Young Peoples Union, depending on the church). Scout Troop 18 held forth in the church recreation hall in Syracuse, and both Bruce and I were members. All three of us started dating within the church (which in both St. Paul and Syracuse was big enough to offer a wide assortment of teenagers from which to strike up acquaintance). Only Margaret, however, eventually married someone from the congregation.

It was Dad who taught us to swim. We learned to cheer for the University of Minnesota Golden Gophers at football games. Dad was not a rabid sports fan, but he once bowled 287, and he played a fair game of baseball. He encouraged us to develop our own interests: Margaret, her music; Bruce, his photography and reptiles; me, my minerals and bicycle trips.

Dad let us borrow the family car—sometimes, I suspect, at more inconvenience to Mother and himself than we knew at the time—and, while not always approving our actions, stood behind us in our rare encounters with the police. (Bruce was stopped, alone in the car with a learner's permit, "just coming home from church." When the police phoned, Dad verified that he knew Bruce to be thus occupied and waited till Bruce's arrival at home to hear the explanation of his route—via Seneca Turnpike, south of town. My own turn came when I was ticketed by a sheriff's deputy for exceeding the speed limit. Dad accompanied me to the police station next day, staked a temporary loan when the fine exceeded my resources, did not growl or shout, but did reinforce, on the way home, the policeman's remark: "Mr. Dahlberg, we've got to slow these teenagers down!")

Mostly, our parents taught by example. Dad did give me a short, informative book to read when I reached puberty, but I learned from observation that happily married people never engage in physical or verbal abuse of each other and are not embarrassed to kiss or embrace in the kitchen or coming in the door. We grew to understand that marriage includes supporting each other in sorrow, sharing moments of contentment, sticking up for each other under attack.

Mother and Dad had a good marriage, one of love and fulfillment. A valentine to Mother from Dad in 1918 was appended to an old reminiscence of Elof's dive into the snow when he went courting. Dad wrote, "May no such mishap come the day I am a bridegroom next September, and if such a misfortune should unhappily occur, please do not imitate my mother in her enjoyment of it. With which plea I give you this little Book of Old Valentines, with the prayer that we may both write in it the most wonderful chapter of all."

They missed each other when they were apart, as they often had to be. Mother's fears that they would see little of each other during a second year of Dad's Northern Baptist Convention presidency were well founded. He had gone on ahead to a Baptist World Congress meeting in Denmark the summer of 1947; she followed with some friends on a different ship (before the days of routine air travel). She notes, "Arriving in Copenhagen, I was taken to the Weber Hotel . . . only to find that Ted was just around the corner. . . . At 1 A.M. I knocked on his door and we had a wonderful reunion after more than a month of separation."[2]

Neither Mother nor Dad publicly criticized us children, though there must have been times when they had to bite their tongues. Mother was frantic when Margaret and her date, Gordon, went canoeing and were not yet home by two in the morning (and the only reason Dad wasn't frantic was because he was in Syracuse and didn't know about it till later). When they did appear, their announcement of their engagement was barely enough to turn her attention away from the night's windstorm and the lake where the two of them had been in a canoe—the same lake in which Dad's nephew Lorimer had lost his life some twenty years before.

On another occasion, after an attractive young lady had visited me during Easter break from college and had departed, Dad happened to be strolling in the same direction as I a couple of days later. He told me she was a "mighty fine, attractive girl" and then continued in a neutral tone, "Just what particular interests do you share in common?" Caught unawares, and reluctant to admit the first that came to mind, I pondered a few minutes as we continued along our walk. There were common interests in music and conversation, but I had difficulty expressing them. "Well," I came up with the best I could after a frantic mental search, "we both like to shake the fizz out of a bottle of pop before we drink it . . ." Dad could not disguise his amusement at this unexpected attribute. He changed the subject, but I got his point.

But a couple years later, when he and Mother returned to Syracuse for a visit (they had moved on to St. Louis, while I remained in medical school) and I introduced them to Lois, the reaction was immediate. The four of us had gone out to eat, and after the meal, Dad pulled me aside and said, "Keith, that's the girl I want for a daughter-in-law!" (We were already secretly engaged, but there was no point in telling him his opinion was too late to influence my choice.) Maybe he instinctively sensed that the chemistry was different, and that this was a good match. There was no ministerial comment about my first meeting Lois on a blind date at a nursing school dance. Dad was not one to argue with God's mysterious ways.

Perhaps the most durable lesson my father ever taught me was during a Christmas visit in St. Louis, when I was in my early twenties. It was a chilly morning as we drove along, and there was a thin layer of new snow on the ground. Railroad crossing lights were flashing up ahead, and I slowed and stopped the car with a slight skid on the slippery street. As we waited in the line of cars while a long freight train rolled past the grade crossing, I turned to say something to Dad and found the seat empty and the car door wide open. Dad was standing on the sidewalk, his hand gently on the shoulder of a swaying drunk who had been about to proceed across the way over which the heavy freight cars were rumbling. The two of them stood there a few moments until the train was past and the way safe. Dad quietly said something to the man, who then stumbled along his way. "What did you say to him?" I asked, as Dad returned to the car. I was hoping to get a capsule instruction in counselling alcoholics.

"Not much to say, when he's as drunk as that," said Dad. "He's not going to remember it. The best you can do sometimes is just keep a man alive, to understand something another day, when his mind is clearer." That stayed in the back of my mind over the years as a primary rule: moralizing and blaming are not first priority; in the moment of crisis, keep the person alive, if you can, and hope for opportunities to help in other ways later.

My parents took the opportunity to visit their children and grandchildren, no matter how far the distance. Just before Christmas in 1961, Lois and I and our three small children greeted Mother and Dad's arrival at Kengtung, Burma, as the twenty-year-old DC-3 of the Union of Burma Airways settled onto the grassy landing strip outside town. It had been a long time since they had seen their grandchildren—medical missionaries did not travel much in those days when there was no replacement doctor—and we all enjoyed the reunion. Dad, of course, was invited by the local church leaders to preach the Christmas sermon that Sunday at Nawng Hpa Baptist, the large brick church on the main mission compound.

I briefed Dad on the local protocol: "Now, Dad, this is where you have to remember that no souls are saved after the first twenty minutes." (This was a long-standing point of friendly argument between us—Dad's sermons averaged thirty-five minutes or more.) "In fact, with the service translated into four languages, you'd better condense it to seven minutes—that way, the sermon altogether will take only thirty-five. The last English-speaking preacher that was here started out with a funny story and by the time it had got through all the translations, his time was up." "—And the humor of the story was lost in translation," I added as an afterthought.

Dad looked dubious about these unfamiliar ground rules, but he downsized his text accordingly, confining it mainly to a Christmas greeting from other churches, worldwide. I remember the row of translators standing at his side: English into Burmese by John Po, then into Lahu by Paul Lewis, on into Shan by Saya David Hsam, and then—would he first go to the window to spit his cud of betel nut?—Rev. Yawtha Chang returned to the line in time to give the translation for the Chinese members.

Both Mother and Dad were instant hits with the five-hundred-member congregation. After church, several elderly Shan women in their turbans and ear-stretching silver earrings came up to stroke Mother's cheeks with amazed soft cries of "Alouu!" "Is that the way they greet people?" Mother asked her daughter-in-law.

"Oh, no," answered Lois, "they had asked me how old you were, and I told them sixty-eight, and they can't believe your smooth skin is real." That night Dad wrote in his diary:

> The music of both the congregation and the choirs was most inspiring. We walked home, talking over the service, and greeting people pleasantly along the way. As we got back to our own room in the guest house, however, Emilie suddenly put her arms around me, and said, "Oh, Teddy, I'm so sorry about this, that after that nice service this morning we've had some bad news!" Things kind of stood still in my mind for a moment, and then she said, "After church we got a message that your brother Henry died of a heart attack!" I was stunned. If it had been my sister Effie, who had not been well, I would have been somewhat prepared for it . . . Emilie left me alone for a few minutes, at my own request, until I was able to pull myself together. . . . Somehow I had always expected that he would outlive us all.[3]

The telegram had taken two days to reach Kengtung. Dad and I drove up to the telegraph office after lunch, where he was able to send ten words for fourteen dollars, hoping the telegram would get there in time for the funeral.

They stayed for two weeks, admiring the hospital's electrical system, which had been installed three years before by Dad's brother-in-law, Laurence Stenger. They attended an outpatient clinic, were invited to tea by the Burmese district court judge, visited with the aunt of the local ruler, toured the Buddhist temples, and, most of all, enchanted their grandchildren. Dad could "wind up his whistle" for them or march around the room with one of them on his shoulder while he sang what they called his "elephant song." Mother could fashion a mouse out of a handkerchief that, if a small child were very careful to pet *gently,* would stay quietly in the palm of her hand and not leap away. Three-year-old John confided to them that he had his bag all packed for when he would visit them the following April.

## Growing Up in a Parsonage

Being children of a nationally known and successful church leader was not always an unmixed blessing. Even though we loved him and respected him, we frequently felt the need for independence. This is probably the reason so many preachers' kids have a reputation as hellions; it is not so much from parental pressure as from the expectations of the church members. I still remember, with mild irritation, an elderly deacon who patted me on the head and told me that I would be a great preacher just like my father. (As I recall, it was that precise moment that crystallized my decision not to enter the ministry.) All three of us children had high regard for our parents, but that did not mean that we did not live our own lives.

Bruce reached draft age in the early part of World War II, did not embrace pacifism, and volunteered for the Tenth Mountain Division (colloquially known as the ski troops), qualifying as a radio operator. By 1943, he was at Camp Hale in Pando, Colorado, racing downslope with an eighty-pound pack on his back. When a need for radio operators developed in the Office of Strategic Services (OSS—the forerunner of the CIA), he volunteered and became attached to the Ninth Army on the German/Dutch border. Bruce, too, fought the idea of the ministry at first, trying his hand as a clerk in the financial world. He later went to seminary, married minister of music Janet Robbins, pastored a church in Brooklyn, New York, and then entered teaching at Smith College, with an active interest in archeological digs in the Middle East. He now has authored an impressive collection of scholarly articles and is professor emeritus of Old Testament at Smith.

Margaret taught school briefly, then married Gordon Torgerson, a ministerial student at the time. At the end of a long and fulfilling professional life, which included its share of conflict on behalf of peace and justice issues, they spent several years in the presidency of Andover Newton Theological School in Newton Centre, Massachusetts. In retirement they served seven years as traveling representatives of the Ministers and Missionaries Benefit Board, visiting and ensuring the well-being of hundreds of retirees each year.

I started out with strong pacifist convictions, registering as a conscientious objector during the Korean War. My viewpoint changed during my years as a doctor in Burma when I saw how much butchery could occur after rebel soldiers had confiscated all guns and dogs and were free to inflict their own malice unopposed. Only after decades of watching guerrilla warfare and the misery it brings, with how little benefit to the citizens in whose name it is waged, have I swung back to Dad's central trust in the message of Christ. Dad never criticized either of his sons' positions on war, though he did not always agree with our basic premises.

In family gatherings, Dad tended to be the center of attention. He did not seek it, but he accepted it. The clan gave him a measure of respect for his work on the national scene and in the pastorate, but that did not always extend to agreement with his views. Family members held a gamut of political beliefs, from conservative Republican to liberal Democrat, and in religion from the agnostic idealism of cousin Phil to the quiet firm faith of Aunt Effie. Conversation was free and friendly at any clan get-together. If Dad ever caused slight family irritation, it was over his habit of suggesting that a matter be prayed about and then proceeding to do so, whether in his own home or someone else's.

Mother and Dad both lived to see all of their twelve living grandchildren. Dad wrote each grandchild a letter when born and occasional letters from exotic stop-offs in his own travels or at milestones in their own lives. He sometimes stopped off for a few days on one of his many auto trips across the country. On such occasions, family rules might have to be slightly bent. As he grew older, Dad was very leisurely at meals, often leaving his fork in midair as he talked—"two and a half hours of half-a-bite and then another story," as the young people put it. Lois or I would finally excuse the teenagers who had other engagements, even though Grandpa had not yet finished his dessert. Even I would sometimes remember a patient at the hospital who should really be checked one more time. Lois, who had no such escape, would later protest in private, "But he's *your* father!"

Margaret's teenagers once agreed to dominate the table conversation nonstop during one of Grandpa's visits so that he would go ahead and eat and finish at the same time as the rest of the family. The scheme failed totally. His fork remained poised in midair while he listened with interest to what his granddaughters were saying.

But when the grandchildren, now adults, reminisce, it is of the times Grandpa went with them to hunt a Christmas tree in the woods or went sledding with them or, at age seventy-seven, showed them how to make "snow angels" by lying in the snow and waving his arms to make the pattern of the wings.

They carry memories of times he helped them. In 1980, when Dad was eighty-seven, Lois and I received a letter from our daughter Pat, then an army lieutenant at Fort Sill, Oklahoma. "Just before I was going to work [Saturday] I got a person-to-person call from Grandpa. He said, 'Patricia— Viola and I are coming for a visit. . . . We'll arrive Tuesday at the bus station at 6 P.M.' What a shock! He hung up after saying he had something he wished to discuss. . . . I figured someone had told him we were living together and we were going to get a talking to. . . . I had to work the three-to-eleven shift the day they arrived, so Dave had to meet them at the bus station without so much as ever laying eyes on them [before]."[4]

It turned out, though, that Dad and Viola knew nothing about the living conditions, until Pat and Dave decided they had better tell them, the next day. They had come to cheer up Pat, who had implied in a letter that she felt frustrated and unprepared for her work. Since Lois and I were overseas, Dad figured it was up to him to help. "You mean you came all the way from Arizona just to see me? Just to cheer me up?" asked Pat wonderingly.

"Well, yes," said Viola. "But now that you've told us, why don't you get married? . . . and quickly," she added as an afterthought. Dad had no intention of railroading them, however. He talked about the pros and cons of getting married now, and when he and Pat were alone, he told her that he thought Dave was a nice man and that she had made a good choice. But there was no pressure.

When Dave and Pat did get married, some months later, it was her Grandpa whom they asked to do the ceremony. Lois and I were back in Idaho by then; Pat had introduced us to Dave, a fine young man, and they had decided to set the date for the end of that same week. A small gathering of friends and family were assembled, and Dave's brother flew up from Missouri to be best man. No one knew Dad's whereabouts at the time—maybe Wyoming, we thought—and it was the Montana State Patrol that finally stopped him and Viola in their travels and told them that they had a wedding to perform over in Idaho.

## Planning Ahead

With increasing age, Dad became more and more concerned about putting his affairs in order. As far back as 1972 he had passed on to us three children the proceeds of a small insurance policy his own father, Elof, had taken out on Dad's life in 1912. This was the policy on which he and Mother had borrowed $1,500 in the 1920s to help build the new church building in Buffalo. In a family letter in 1972, Dad wrote about that church and his investment in it:

> The neighborhood has deteriorated terribly, but the church is still carrying on a courageous ministry, so that the light we dreamed of "lighting on the hill" still shines. Mother and I ultimately got the $1500 paid off, and we considered

it to be one of the best investments we ever made, even though it meant scrap-
ing the bottom of the barrel financially at the time. If the enclosed check can
be of help . . . in finishing the education of your children and easing the way
into the future, I feel that this will be an equally fine investment. . . . I believe
the four most important books in any Christian home are the Bible, the hymn-
book, the checkbook and the pocketbook. It is the last two that give substance
to the faith proclaimed in the first two.[5]

Ten years later, approaching ninety, Dad sent us a copy of his will and
directions for disposing of his assets. Arizona law requires that the estate
executor be an Arizona resident; he nominated a local bank. The twenty-
three notebooks containing his diaries would go to the American Baptist
Historical Society. In addition, he had a large number of sermons and letters. He did not wish to inflict the task of sorting and preserving them on
anyone since he himself had, through the years, frequently been burdened
in that manner by widows of ministers. (One sensed that he hoped his
papers would be preserved in some manner, and ultimately they have
been.) There were a few pieces of furniture and heirlooms, other than what
Viola would use, that we should divide up when the time came. He closed
the letter with a quote from his father, Elof: "Considering our ups and
downs, we regard our children's educations, all developing a good honest
character to render service to mankind to be our most valuable assets."[6]

During this period, a number of people realized the presence of a walking repository of nearly a century of history among them and made efforts
to record some of it on tape. Dad was happy to oblige. "There are two
advantages to growing this old," he told one of his interviewers with a
smile. "For one thing, hardly anyone else is still around to contradict me.
For another, my memory has improved with age so much that I can now
remember things that never even happened!" (Actually, I have found that
the material on Dad's taped interviews agrees remarkably well with written records of the times in most cases.)

A Baptist journalist, Nancy Neal, asked Dad in 1981 what he felt his
strong points had been. He reflected a minute: "I rather like presiding.
Presiding—guiding—is a God-given gift." And his failures? He replied,
"Some sermons [for] which people were not yet prepared. I got too impa-
tient and went ahead."[7] To this, some of his colleagues might have added
his failure to ever say anything bad about someone who had asked him
for a job reference. Everyone was always "a great scout," or some equiv-
alent term, with rarely a real assessment of the candidate's competence as
a minister.[8]

Although Dad continued to write to many friends and former parishioners, more and more of his correspondence piled up unanswered. On one July visit, I found several hundred Christmas cards still awaiting reply—very uncharacteristic of Dad. His physical health remained remarkably good for his age, but he had increasing difficulty with memory. He could name the people in a 1912 photograph. He could recite the Twenty-third Psalm accurately along with his grandsons Jamie and John. He had increasing difficulty, however, in recalling what had been said five minutes previously. It became increasingly apparent, after medical tests, that he was developing Alzheimer's disease.

I do not know what Dad would have done without Viola. He wanted to remain among his friends in Phoenix. We children and grandchildren visited—one or another of us making the trip to Phoenix every month or two—but it was Viola who walked with him, saw that he got to meals, comforted him with her daily companionship. He often fell, finally becoming too weak to manage at home. He entered the health facility at Orangewood at age ninety-two, living out another year of gradually failing strength.

Ever since I can remember, Dad had stated his intent to live to the age of 107, to experience life in three centuries. (He dismissed the suggestion that the twenty-first century would not start until a week after he reached 108.) On one of our last visits, I was sitting with him while he slowly made his way through lunch. There was a long pause in the spoon's progress. "Eat up, Dad," I gently urged him. "Remember, you want to reach 107."

The spoon paused again; his eyes turned toward me, considering this apparently new idea. And he said, firmly, "Why, that's the craziest idea I ever heard of."

In the end, Dad developed pneumonia and passed away quietly and rather quickly on 6 September 1986 at the age of ninety-three.

# Epilogue

Dad's obituary appeared in many periodicals, from the *Kellogg (Idaho) Evening News* to the *New York Times*.[1] Philip Jenks, editor of the *American Baptist,* summed up well:

> Everything about Dahlberg—his pacifism, his social activism, his teaching, his preaching—focused on the need for individuals to turn their lives over to Jesus and to live as disciples. His parishioners and many friends—even those who disagreed with his social stands—always understood that. . . . He was great because he taught us all how to find our fellow human beings wherever they were and give them a simple message: "Stay close to the Lord. Read the Bible. Remember what you learn in church."[2]

Other than a few personal possessions and memorabilia, and a large quantity of personal papers, Edwin T. Dahlberg left no estate. He left a legacy of a different quality. In Dad's eulogy, Richard Ice said, "He had a dream, and he could not forget it; it was always out ahead of him."[3] He had a vision of a world at peace. Being unable to map the exact route to that world did not deter him—the goal is often seen before the path is clear.

Dad knew that many routes were dead ends: Hatred breeds vengeance. Military might leads to escalation, impoverishing nations when it does not totally destroy them. "Holy wars"—be they called crusades, jihads, or revolutions—by their vindictiveness make a mockery of the religion they claim to serve.

"We have not been satisfied to say glibly, 'Christ is the answer,'" Dad said. "We know that Christ is the answer, but we have tried to work out the human equations between the problem and the answer, so that it might be demonstrated how the answer in Christ is to be found."[4]

Dad knew that there would always be honest differences in belief. He often quoted Count Hermann Keyserling, who said that humans never really settle such differences; they must rise above them to a higher level of responsibility. Thus—

There will always be argument over "interpretation" versus "inerrancy" of Scripture. The argument must not obscure the reality of God in the world.

There will probably always be the politics of the right and the left. Disputes and political maneuvering must not paralyze the country (or world) from improving the lot of its citizens.

There will inevitably be conflicts of national or racial interest. There are ways to settle them without justifying slaughter.

Reconciliation has not yet been reached in any of these arenas. In the present state of the world, there is still a place for armed police, he acknowledged. Given the present low level of skills in international diplomacy, it is probably not yet the time to disband armies. Keeping the vision alive, however, is essential to finding the path. Dad devoted his life to this purpose, and there are many like him.

To those who would dismiss Dad and people like him as visionaries out of touch with the facts, I suggest a few facts to ponder:

Humanity is in fact capable of humaneness. The aftermath of World War I saddled the losers with war reparations debts that, however just they may have been, caused deep economic depression and inflation in Germany and prepared the nation for the likes of Adolf Hitler. After World War II, the victors took pains not to destroy Japan and promoted economic recovery in Europe with the Marshall Plan, despite complaints about the expense of foreign aid. And the year following the end of World War II saw the establishment of the United Nations' Children's Fund (UNICEF), the Cooperative for American Relief to Everywhere (CARE), and the Centers for Disease Control and Prevention (CDC).[5]

But war is still with us and is in some ways more vicious than ever. It is said that the most numerous deaths in modern war are among children:

> Two million children died in wars in the past decade [1985 to 1995]. War claimed the lives of more children than soldiers. An additional 4.5 million were disabled and 12 million were left homeless. Over 100 million mines are in the ground and continue to ruin the lives of children even at the end of hostilities. While children have always been at risk of unintended violence during conflict, wars today often target children. In 1988, it was estimated that 200,000 children younger than 16 years were actually soldiers. Science has provided lighter weapons, and children follow directions! In addition, the fact that children die of diarrhea, measles, malnutrition, and lack of sanitation in Rwanda, Burundi, Sudan, Liberia, and other areas exceeds our comprehension.[6]

The vision of a peaceful world does not disappear with the death of the visionary. Whether or not Gandhi or Aung San Suu Kyi or Martin Luther King Jr. or the peacemakers of a future generation realize their goal in their lifetime, the vision remains, indestructible, for all of us to seek. Resolving conflict without resort to war happens through people who will it to be so, who bring conflicts into honest, open discussion, with the interests of both sides considered, until agreement is reached. It will come in a series of achievements and failures. But it will come. It is part of the vision of God's purpose for humankind.

The memorial service for Edwin T. Dahlberg was a time of celebration of life well lived. Friends and family filled the chapel at Orangewood on the morning of 12 September 1986 as the organist played a prelude medley of Dad's favorite hymns. The family had not encouraged flowers, but there were many, ranging from large bouquets of roses to a small glass jar holding a handful of daisies from his great-grandchildren.

The service had no sermon, just a number of people's memories.[7] No one dwelt much on the organizations he had led, except to recall his bringing the remaining Northern Baptist churches together in unity forty years earlier, after some had left to go their separate way. Most of us remembered personal things—his sense of humor, his helpfulness. Each of us three children spoke briefly. Margaret was the last, closing by leading the assemblage in a verse of an old hymn:

> Then let our songs abound, let every tear be dry;
> We're marching through Emmanuel's ground, we're marching through Emmanuel's ground,
> To fairer worlds on high, to fairer worlds on high.
> We're marching to Zion, beautiful, beautiful Zion;
> We're marching upward to Zion, the beautiful City of God.[8]

There is no grave site for Edwin T. Dahlberg. Both he and Mother, on their own initiative, willed their bodies to science.

Mother has a memorial garden at Orangewood in Phoenix, Arizona.

Dad is memorialized in a bronze plaque at the American Baptist Assembly at Green Lake, Wisconsin:

Edwin T. Dahlberg
Born: December 27, 1892
Died: September 6, 1986
"BLESSED ARE THE PEACEMAKERS"

# Notes

Most of the documents cited below, unless otherwise mentioned, are in the author's personal files. With the exception of family letters, most are also in the archives of the American Baptist Historical Society, 1106 South Goodman Street, Rochester, N.Y. 14620-2532 (hereinafter abbreviated ABHS). Edwin T. Dahlberg's papers are collected in archive section 1026. Some of his sermons and other papers are still in the process of being sorted at the home of Bruce T. Dahlberg in Northampton, Massachusetts.

## Preface
1. From a letter in Bruce Dahlberg's files.

## Chapter One: Sweden
Although the conversations in the first two chapters are speculative, the content is consistent with historical fact, based on writings left by Elof Dahlberg and several interviews with Edwin T. Dahlberg (hereinafter abbreviated ETD) recorded on cassette tapes from 1974 onward.
1. ETD, interview by Viola Dahlberg, tape recording, 1981, Phoenix. ETD originally heard the story from the man who was the infant in the incident, which reportedly happened in the 1850s. The man was a member of ETD's church in St. Paul.
2. Elof Dahlberg, unpublished memoir, 1929.
3. ETD, "Our Witness at Christmas," sermon delivered at Delmar Street Baptist Church, St. Louis, 20 December 1953.
4. ETD, Viola Dahlberg interview.
5. Ibid.
6. ETD, interview by Dorothy Cordwell, tape recording, 1974, Kellogg, Idaho.
7. Ibid.

## Chapter Two: Minnesota
1. Chapter 2 is based on the taped interviews of ETD by Viola Dahlberg and Dorothy Cordwell cited above and on Elof Dahlberg's unpublished memoir, 1929.

## Chapter Three: Edwin
1. ETD, interview by Dorothy Cordwell, tape recording, 1974, Kellogg, Idaho.

2. ETD, family letter, 24 February 1982; translation of poem and obituary by ETD.

3. ETD, Cordwell interview.

4. Ibid.

5. ETD, family letter, 20 August 1959.

6. ETD, family letter, 20 March 1961.

7. ETD, "My Religious Autobiography" (paper written in seminary, ca. 1916), ABHS.

8. Ibid.

9. Clarissa Start, "Dr. Dahlberg's National Pastorate," 11 April 1959. Reprinted with permission of *St. Louis Post-Dispatch,* copyright 1997.

10. ETD, Cordwell interview.

11. ETD, "The Universal Invitation," sermon delivered at Delmar Street Baptist Church, St. Louis, 10 February 1957.

12. ETD, "My Religious Autobiography."

13. ETD, "Why I Chose the Ministry" (address at McEndree College, St. Louis, Missouri, 9 October 1959), reprinted in *St. Louis Globe Democrat,* 11 October 1959.

14. Ibid.; also ETD, general Christmas letter, 1980, reminiscing on events seventy years before.

15. Walter E. Orthwein, "Follower of Christ and Leader of Men," *St. Louis Globe Democrat,* 8 December 1957.

16. Henri Nepven, letters to ETD, 9 April and 7 May 1910, ABHS.

17. ETD, interview by Beverly Davison, tape recording, 1982, Green Lake, Wis., ABHS.

18. ETD, "Why I Chose the Ministry."

19. ETD, "My Religious Autobiography."

20. Henry Dahlberg, "What Henry Found," unpublished memoir, 1913.

21. ETD, "My Religious Autobiography."

22. Gordon Torgersen, "Dahlberg Ecumenical Lecture," tape recording, 31 August 1988, Colgate Rochester Divinity School, Rochester, N.Y.

23. ETD, interview by John Skoglund, tape recording, 1972, Green Lake, Wis., ABHS.

24. Torgersen, "Dahlberg Ecumenical Lecture."

25. Ibid.

26. ETD, Skoglund interview.

27. Torgersen, "Dahlberg Ecumenical Lecture."

28. ETD, letter to Maline Broberg, 24 September 1984.

29. ETD, letter to Martha S. Miller, 17 December 1981, based on three meditations on the subject "My Experiences as a Conscientious Objector to War," Baptist Peace Fellowship Conference, Snow Ranch, Colo., August 1976.

30. Ibid.

31. Torgersen, "Dahlberg Ecumenical Lecture."

## Chapter Four: Pastor

1. Emilie Loeffler to ETD, series of letters, summer 1917.
2. ETD, letter to a Potsdam congregation member, 2 April 1918, ABHS.
3. ETD, letter to Potsdam church, 18 December 1918, ABHS.
4. ETD, letter to J. Martin, 25 March 1918, ABHS.
5. ETD, "Why I Chose the Ministry" (address at McEndree College, St. Louis, Missouri, 9 October 1959), reprinted in *St. Louis Globe Democrat,* 11 October 1959.
6. ETD, family letter, 25 September 1972.
7. Gordon H. Baker, letter to ETD, 23 December 1923, ABHS.
8. ETD, letter replying to Gordon H. Baker, 22 January 1924, ABHS.
9. Gordon Torgersen, "Dahlberg Ecumenical Lecture," tape recording, 31 August 1988, Colgate Rochester Divinity School, Rochester, N.Y.
10. Chris E. Schurmen, editorial, *St. Paul Times,* 7 February 1931, quoted in *A Church in Lowertown* (written on 125th anniversary of founding of First Baptist Church, St. Paul) (St. Paul: Mason, 1975), 134.
11. Torgersen, "Dahlberg Ecumenical Lecture."
12. *A Church in Lowertown,* 122.
13. Torgersen, "Dahlberg Ecumenical Lecture."
14. Ibid.
15. Ibid.
16. ETD, letter to congregation of First Baptist Church of St. Paul, 1 January 1939, ABHS.

## Chapter Five: Syracuse

1. ETD, "The Minister and War," Peace Council broadcast, radio station WSYR (Syracuse, N.Y.), 6 May 1940, 10:45 P.M., ABHS.
2. W. Brewster Hall, letter to ETD, 25 June 1940, ABHS.
3. Levi Chapman, letter to ETD, 3 July 1940, ABHS.
4. ETD, reply to Brewster Hall, ca. 1 July 1940, ABHS.
5. Gordon Torgersen, "Dahlberg Ecumenical Lecture," tape recording, 31 August 1988, Colgate Rochester Divinity School, Rochester, N.Y.
6. I attended high school during the 1940s when the program of prayer and Bible reading was developed in Syracuse. Each day, a different student was assigned to choose a passage of Scripture and read it. By far the most frequently chosen Bible passage was Psalm 134 because students had quickly discovered that it had only three verses.
7. ETD, interview by Viola Dahlberg, tape recording, 1981, Phoenix.
8. John Schroeder, letter to author, 26 July 1997.
9. Woodrow W. Clark, letter to author, 26 July 1997.
10. Author's personal recollection.
11. Ernest Bowden, *Syracuse Post-Standard,* n.d., ABHS.
12. ETD, *Youth in the Homes of Tomorrow* (Valley Forge, Pa.: Judson Press, 1934), ABHS.

13. ETD, letter, 26 March 1946, ABHS.

14. Torgersen, "Dahlberg Ecumenical Lecture."

15. Fred Allen, letter to ETD, 8 August 1950, ABHS.

## Chapter Six: National Leader

1. Jawaharlal Nehru (address to Third Assembly of World Council of Churches, New Delhi, December 1961), as quoted by ETD, interview by Beverly Davison, tape recording, 1982, Green Lake, Wis., ABHS.

2. For further information on the Baptist contribution to the Bill of Rights, see O. K. and Marjorie Armstrong's excellent account *The Indomitable Baptists* (Camden City, N.Y.: Doubleday, 1967), 1-16.

3. Acts 16:31, KJV.

4. Matthew 6:10, KJV.

5. Gordon Torgersen, interview by author, 16 December 1995.

6. Clipping from unidentified Grand Rapids, Mich., newspaper, May 1946, ABHS.

7. *Yearbook of the Northern Baptist Convention* (Philadelphia: The Judson Press, 1946), ABHS.

8. Ibid.

9. ETD, "The Unfailing Lamp of God" (address to Northern Baptist Convention, Grand Rapids, Mich., May 1946).

10. Report of the 1946 Northern Baptist Convention, *Missions,* June 1946.

11. ETD, interview by L. Doward McBain, tape recording, 1972, ABHS.

12. Associated Press release, 1 November 1946, ABHS.

13. Dr. Murk, letter to ETD, (undated) 1946, ABHS.

14. W. B. Riley, letter to ETD, 20 May 1947, ABHS.

15. W. Abernethy, letter to ETD, 25 June 1946, ABHS.

16. C. Oscar Johnson, letter to ETD, 12 March 1947, ABHS.

17. Norman T. Mears, letter to ETD, 20 February 1947, ABHS.

18. Earl V. Pierce, letter to ETD, 23 January 1947, ABHS.

19. ETD, "President's Forum," general letter to Northern Baptists, February 1947, ABHS.

20. The German philosopher Count Hermann Keyserling (1880-1946), as quoted in ETD, "President's Forum."

21. Harold B. Porterfield, letter to ETD, 23 February 1947, ABHS.

22. ETD, letter replying to Harold B. Porterfield, 8 March 1947, author's files.

23. *Syracuse Post-Standard,* 13 January 1947.

24. W. B. Riley, letter to ETD, 10 May 1947, ABHS.

25. Gordon Torgersen, "Dahlberg Ecumenical Lecture," tape recording, 31 August 1988, Colgate Rochester Divinity School, Rochester, N.Y.

26. Roger Frederickson, personal interview by author, July 1996.

27. ETD, "Northern Baptists—Turn Northward!" (address before Northern Baptist Convention, Atlantic City, N.J., 20 May 1947). Because of a primitive and faulty wire tape recorder, this speech was not successfully recorded at the time. The

original manuscript may be among as yet unsorted sermons in Bruce T. Dahlberg's files, Northampton, Massachusetts. The quotation is taken from *Baptist New Yorker,* June 1947, ABHS.

28. *Yearbook of the Northern Baptist Convention* (Philadelphia: The Judson Press, 1947), ABHS.

29. ETD, interview by Nancy Dahlberg Neal, tape recording, 1981, Green Lake, Wis., ABHS. Although ETD did not name the motion in the 1981 interview, the minutes of the 1947 Northern Baptist Convention in Atlantic City list only one withdrawn motion: that the Northern Baptist Convention recognize the withdrawal of the Conservative Baptist Association. Evidently there was still some hope for reconciliation. The formal incorporation of the Conservative Baptist Association took place in 1948.

30. "What Does a Convention President Do?" *Crusader,* February 1948, ABHS.

31. Meeting notices, *Watchman Examiner,* 1 May 1947, 424; 8 May 1947, 466; ABHS.

32. *Yearbook of the Northern Baptist Convention* (Philadelphia: The Judson Press, 1948), ABHS.

33. *Milwaukee Journal,* 30 May 1948, ABHS.

34. ETD, interview by Viola Dahlberg, tape recording, 1981, Phoenix.

35. Report on Toronto WCC meeting, 8-15 July 1950, *Missions,* August 1950, ABHS.

36. ETD, August diary, 1951, ABHS.

37. ETD, family letter, 12 August 1951.

38. ETD, diary, 1951, ABHS.

39. Martin Niemöller, memorandum to Fellowship of Reconciliation, 21 July 1950, ABHS.

## Chapter Seven: St. Louis

1. The Northern Baptist Convention changed its name to American Baptist Convention in 1950, and in 1972 to American Baptist Churches in the U.S.A.

2. ETD, family letter, 29 January 1951.

3. ETD, letter to Paul and Helen Compton, 4 October 1951.

4. ETD, family letter, 19 March 1951.

5. ETD, family letter, 25 March 1951.

6. ETD, family letter, 20 February 1951.

7. ETD, letter to author, 17 November 1951.

8. ETD, letter to author, 30 May 1959.

9. ETD, "The Gospel and the Political and Social Order," sermon delivered at Delmar Street Baptist Church, St. Louis, 6 February 1955.

10. ETD, "The Universal Invitation," sermon delivered at Delmar Street Baptist Church, St. Louis, 12 February 1957.

11. ETD, "When Machines Do Our Work," sermon delivered at Delmar Street Baptist Church, St. Louis, 4 September 1955.

12. ETD, "Why I Chose the Ministry" (address at McEndree College, St. Louis, 9 October 1959), reprinted in *St. Louis Globe Democrat,* 11 October 1959.

13. ETD, "God of the Unknown Way," sermon delivered at Delmar Street Baptist Church, St. Louis, 9 September 1956.

14. ETD, letter to author, 3 January 1953.

15. ETD, "This Is the Victory," sermon delivered at Delmar Street Baptist Church, St. Louis, 20 January 1957, emphasis added.

16. Emilie L. Dahlberg, interview by Ruth E. Philson, *Worcester (Mass.) Telegram & Gazette,* 5 March 1963, 18.

17. Bruce T. Dahlberg, quoted by ETD, family letter, 19 November 1962.

18. LaRue (Larry) Loughhead, letter shared with author, July 1997.

19. Lois Brackman, letter to author, 23 July 1997.

20. ETD, family letter, 6 February 1961.

21. The visit to my family in Burma is told about in chapter 11.

22. ETD, "Baptist Pastor's View," written for *Newspaper Enterprise Association,* New York, 21 September 1962, ABHS.

23. ETD, family letter, 25 May 1961.

24. ETD, family letter, 10 June 1961.

25. ETD, family letter, 19 November 1962.

26. ETD, *I Pick Up Hitchhikers* (Valley Forge, Pa.: Judson Press, 1978), 104.

## Chapter Eight: National Council of Churches

1. James Russell Lowell, "Once to Every Man and Nation," stanza 2.

2. ETD, "The Baptist Witness in the Ecumenical Movement" (address to the American Baptist Convention, Cincinnati, 13 June 1958).

3. Clarissa Start, "Dr. Dahlberg's National Pastorate," 11 April 1959. Reprinted with permission of *St. Louis Post-Dispatch,* copyright 1997.

4. *Christian Century,* 13 December 1950.

5. Senator Joseph R. McCarthy (R-Wis.) announced in 1950 that he had a list of 57 known communists employed by the U.S. State Department. He later claimed the number was 205. Reelected to the Senate in 1952, he attained the chairmanship of the Senate Permanent Subcommittee on Investigations. Although he was never able to produce evidence of subversion, many jobs were lost and many reputations destroyed in this era of McCarthyism. His downfall came in 1954 during thirty-six days of nationally televised hearings on the army (McCarthy had included President Eisenhower in his list of alleged traitors); the Senate removed him from the subcommittee chairmanship and officially censured him. His influence then dwindled, though some of his followers continued to believe his claims even after his death in 1957.

6. ETD, "The Task Before Us," inaugural address to NCC General Assembly, St. Louis, 6 December 1957. The reference to "Jesus' point-four program" is an analogy to President Harry Truman's 1949 State of the Union speech, wherein Truman proposed his "point-four program," an economic plan of U.S. foreign policy that included (1) supporting the United Nations, (2) continuing programs for world

economic recovery, (3) pursuing agreements for mutual defense against aggressors, and (4) using U.S. scientific and industrial progress to aid underdeveloped areas of the world.

7. Dwight D. Eisenhower, "Chance for Peace" (address in Washington, D.C., 16 April 1953), courtesy of the Eisenhower Library, Abilene, Kansas. The speech is published in full in *Public Papers of the Presidents of the United States: Dwight D. Eisenhower, 1953* (Washington, D.C.: Government Printing Office, 1960), 179-88 (quotation from p. 182).

8. ETD, "Protestant Contributions to Patriotism" (address at Plattsburgh, N.Y., 2 August 1959), summarized in letter to author, 3 August 1959.

9. ETD, family letter, 16 February 1959.

10. ETD, family letter, 21 February 1959.

11. ETD, family letter, 24 October 1960.

12. ETD, letter to Gordon and Margaret Torgersen, 13 October 1958. Permission for use obtained from Gordon Torgersen.

13. Dispute over Quemoy Island and the nearby Matsu Islands, in the Strait of Formosa, nearly started war between mainland China and the U.S. in 1958. Communist China had driven General Chiang Kai-shek's Nationalist Chinese army off the mainland in 1949–50, and the latter then took over the island of Formosa (Taiwan), creating in essence two Chinese governments. Communist China's forces threatened invasion in 1958 by shelling the Nationalist-held Quemoy and the Matsus; the United States brought up naval forces as a countermeasure. Hence, Eisenhower was pleased with the two Chinese governments' cease-fire agreement.

14. ETD, letter to Torgersons, 13 October 1958.

15. ETD, family letters, 4 September and 14 September 1959.

16. ETD, "The Adversary in the Way," sermon delivered at Delmar Street Baptist Church, St. Louis, 13 September 1959.

17. ETD, family letter, 15 November 1960.

18. ETD, "Protestantism in Puerto Rico," sermon delivered at Delmar Street Baptist Church, St. Louis, 26 April 1959.

19. ETD, letter to Robert and Dorothy Cordwell, 23 December 1957.

20. Ibid.

21. ETD, general newsletter, 8 January 1959, ABHS, box 1026-1.

22. ETD, "Marooned in Morocco," sermon delivered at Delmar Street Baptist Church, St. Louis, 18 January 1959.

23. ETD, travel diary, 21–24 December 1959. ABHS, box 1026-39.

24. Ibid.

25. Quoted in Start, "Dr. Dahlberg's National Pastorate." See chapter 8, note 3.

26. ETD, "The Churches and the National Conscience" (address, Hartford, Conn., 24 February 1959); also summarized in *New York Times,* 25 February 1959, p. 1.

27. ETD, family letter, 30 January 1970.

28. ETD, family letter, 10 October 1960.

29. ETD, family letter, 29 July 1960.

30. ETD, family letter, 22 July 1960.

31. *Oklahoma City Times,* 17 February 1960, p. 1.

32. *Philadelphia Inquirer,* 18 February 1960.

33. Lackland Military Training Center, *Air Reserve Center Training Manual,* 45-0050, increment 5, vol. 7, student text (Mitchell Air Force Base, N.Y.: Continental Air Command, 1960), 15.14; ABHS, box 1026-28. The Revised Standard Version of the Bible was completed in 1952 by the Division of Christian Education of the NCC and published by Thomas Nelson, Inc. (Nashville). It is one of the earlier of many translations of the Bible into modern-day English to appear in the twentieth century.

34. Lackland Military Training Center, *Air Reserve Center Training Manual,* 15.4; ABHS, box 1026-28.

35. ETD, family letter, 22 February 1960.

36. ETD, family letter, 29 February 1960.

37. *Congressional Record,* 86th Cong., 19 April 1960, vol. 106, pp. 7669-7705.

38. National Council of the Churches of Christ in the U.S.A., . . . *the Truth* (New York: NCC, 1960), ABHS, box 1026-28. Hereinafter cited as ". . . the Truth."

39. *Minneapolis Tribune,* 19 February 1960, ABHS.

40. ETD, family letter, 22 February 1960.

41. ETD, family letter, 2 July 1960.

42. Ibid.; also ETD, family letter, 28 June 1960.

43. Gordon Torgersen, "Dahlberg Ecumenical Lecture," tape recording, 31 August 1988, Colgate Rochester Divinity School, Rochester, N.Y.; also LaRue (Larry) Loughhead, letter to author, July 1997.

44. Billy James Hargis, phone interview with author, 21 August 1997. In this conversation Dr. Hargis stated that he did not mind my quoting the two of his pamphlets that led to the statements in the Air Force manual. "I have no objections to that," he said. "Your dad was one of the best friendships I ever had. A nice guy. . . . Your dad was not an ultraliberal, not a liar, not an out-and-out liberal. . . . [He and I] would discuss, not argue." Their long discussion that afternoon in Hargis's hotel room ended when a fire happened to break out elsewhere in the hotel. Hargis recollects that his wife, Betty, their daughters, and the nanny had gone off to the zoo, but his small son was napping in a nearby room. He and Dad led the boy down the smoke-filled hall. Neither says what the news reporters gathered with the firemen below had to say about this unexpected and unlikely trio descending the fire escape.

45. ETD, family letter, 9 June 1960.

46. ETD, family letter, 4 June 1960.

47. ETD received four honorary degrees: D.D., Keuka College (N.Y.), 1939; D.D., Kalamazoo College (Mich.), 1947; LL.D. Franklin College (Ind.), 1959; and D.D., Denison University (Ohio), 1960.

48. ETD, family letter, 16 October 1960. The Gandhi Peace Award was given by the Society for Promoting Enduring Peace (New York City). In this first year of its annual presentation, the award was given jointly to Dahlberg and to Eleanor Roosevelt.

49. Torgersen, "Dahlberg Ecumenical Lecture."

50. ETD, family letter, 2 January 1961.

51. ETD, family letter, 22 September 1961. To give some sense of proportion to the conflict, the American Baptist Churches in the U.S.A. publishes a biennial list of their member churches who ask to be disassociated from support of the NCC. *The Directory of the American Baptist Churches 1996* shows about 11 percent are on this list. None of the twenty-two current American Baptist congregations in Columbus are on it. The other 89 percent, nationwide, do contribute financial support to the NCC. See *Directory of the American Baptist Churches 1996* (Valley Forge, Pa.: American Baptist Churches in the U.S.A., 1996), 189.

52. ETD, family letter, 7 October 1961.

53. . . .*the Truth* (New York: NCC, 1960), 30, ABHS, box 1026-28. The Circuit Riders were a group of Methodist laypeople (without any official connection to the Methodist Church) organized in 1951 in Cincinnati, Ohio, to "oppose socialism and communism," led by Myers G. Lowman.

54. ETD, "Statement by Edwin T. Dahlberg" (address at 136th Annual Ohio Baptist Convention, Columbus, 12 October 1961), reported in *Crusader,* October 1961, 7, ABHS.

55. Senator Patrick McCarran (D) of Nevada sponsored the Immigration and Nationality Act of 1952, promoting the exclusion of "security risks" from the United States.

56. ETD, family letter, 15 October 1961.

57. Many churches have investigated the NCC for themselves, one example being Fifth Avenue Baptist Church of Huntington, West Virginia, which mimeographed a seven-page report of their committee's yearlong study and findings: Charles A. Brown, chairman, report submitted 16 October 1968, ABHS.

## Chapter Nine: The Vietnam War Years

1. ETD, Christmas letter, 1963.

2. Gordon Torgersen, quoting Dr. King's letter of 12 December 1960, in "Dahlberg Ecumenical Lecture," tape recording, 31 August 1988, Colgate Rochester Divinity School, Rochester, N.Y. The original letter is in Bruce T. Dahlberg's files, Northampton, Massachusetts.

3. ETD, "The Task Before Us," inaugural address to NCC General Assembly, St. Louis, 6 December 1957.

4. ETD, family letter, 15 May 1965.

5. Ibid.

6. The twelve American members of the tour were all members of the Peace Commission of the Fellowship of Reconciliation (Nyack, N.Y.); two Europeans joined the group in Asia. As listed in ETD's diary of July 1965, included in the group were Dr. Harold A. Bosley, minister of Christ (Methodist) Church, New York City, and former dean of Duke University Divinity School; Rt. Rev. William Crittenden, (Episcopal) bishop of Erie, Pennsylvania, and vice president of the NCC; Dr. Edwin T. Dahlberg, past president of the NCC and of the American Baptist Convention; Dr.

Dana McLean Greeley, president of the Unitarian-Universalist Association of America; Alfred Hassler, executive secretary of the Fellowship of Reconciliation; Elmira Kendricks, president of the National Student Christian Federation; Rev. James M. Lawson, minister of Centenary Methodist Church, Memphis, Tennessee; Dr. Howard Schomer, president of Chicago Theological Seminary; Mrs. Howard Schomer of the Women's International League for Peace and Freedom; Rev. Annalee Stewart, former president of the Women's International League for Peace and Freedom; Rabbi Jacob Weinstein, president of the Central Conference of American Rabbis (and the only member whose organization had authorized him to speak for the organization as a whole); Rt. Rev. Edward Murray, pastor of Sacred Heart Parish, Roslindale, Massachusetts; Pastor Martin Niemöller, copresident of the WCC, Weisbaden, Germany; and Pasteur Andre Trocme, St. Servais Reformed Church, Geneva, Switzerland.

7. ETD, travel diary, July 1965, ABHS, box 1026-39.

8. Ibid.

9. ETD, family letter, 12 July 1965.

10. Ibid.; also ETD, travel diary, July 1965.

11. ETD, travel diary, July 1965.

12. ETD, letter to Rev. Lawrence Horst, 29 September 1965, ABHS, box 1026-20.

13. ETD, letter to Mrs. Byron Johnson, Denver, 29 September 1965, ABHS, box 1026-20.

14. Walter A. McClenighan (for UN Association of Greater Phoenix), letter to ETD, 6 October 1965, ABHS, box 1026-20.

15. Paul C. Allen, "Viet Nam: Two Points of View," *Crusader,* February 1966, 2-5, ABHS.

16. Aleksei Kosygin, interview by James Reston, *New York Times,* 7 December 1965, cited by Allen, "Viet Nam: Two Points of View."

17. "Letters to the Editor," *Crusader,* April 1966, 10-11, ABHS.

18. Paul C. Allen, letter to James H. Mowe, 1966, ABHS.

19. ETD, family letter, 27 February 1965.

20. ETD, family letter, 27 August 1961.

21. ETD, family letter, 15 November 1969.

22. ETD, letter to Internal Revenue Service, 5 April 1971.

23. Paul Lewis, letter to author, 24 January 1997.

24. ETD, handwritten note (evidently a first draft), April 1973, ABHS.

## Chapter Ten: Pastor Emeritus

1. This event is from Dad's records and is told here because clergy who forget their calling and prey on their parishioners have become an increasing and alarming problem in the late twentieth century. Nothing is gained by stating the time and place.

2. Richard Deats, letter to author, 26 February 1997.

3. ETD, Christmas letter, 1976, Maline Broberg collection.

4. ETD, family letter, 1 January 1977.

5. ETD, *Youth in the Homes of Tomorrow* (Valley Forge, Pa.: Judson Press, 1934), ABHS.

6. Robert Remington, personal recollection in interview with author, Rochester, N.Y., 1995.

7. Keith Dahlberg, family letter, 19 February 1977.

8. To allay confusion about Dad finding my family in widely scattered parts of the world, we worked in Kengtung, Burma, 1957-62; Mae Sariang, Thailand, 1963-67, and again 1977-81; I was in medical practice in northern Idaho, 1967-77 and from 1982 onward.

9. ETD, ed., *Heralds of the Evangel* (St. Louis: Bethany Press, 1965).

10. ETD, "Psalm of the Sugarbush," unpublished, n.d., ABHS.

11. ETD, *I Pick Up Hitchhikers* (Valley Forge, Pa.: Judson Press, 1978).

## Chapter Eleven: Family

1. ETD, family letter, 24 March 1961.

2. Emilie L. Dahlberg, diary, 28 July 1947.

3. ETD, diary, December 1961.

4. Patricia Cordier, letter to author, 13 August 1980.

5. ETD, family letter, 25 September 1972.

6. ETD, family letter, 10 May 1982.

7. ETD, interview by Nancy Dahlberg Neal, tape recording, 1981, Green Lake, Wis., ABHS.

8. Gordon Torgersen, "Dahlberg Ecumenical Lecture," tape recording, 31 August 1988, Colgate Rochester Divinity School, Rochester, N.Y.

## Epilogue

1. *New York Times,* 9 September 1986, sec. B, p. 6.

2. Philip E. Jenks, "Edwin T. Dahlberg: A Good Neighbor," *The American Baptist,* January-February 1987, 14-15.

3. Richard Ice, eulogy for ETD (memorial service, speaking for American Baptist Churches in the U.S.A. and for the National Council of the Churches of Christ in the U.S.A.).

4. ETD, "The Task before Us," inaugural address to NCC General Assembly, St. Louis, 6 December 1957).

5. William H. Foege, *Journal of the American Medical Association* 275 (1996): 1846.

6. Ibid., quoting C. Bellamy, *The State of the World's Children 1996* (New York: Oxford University Press, 1995).

7. The memorial service was preserved on cassette tape by Viola Dahlberg.

8. Isaac Watts, "We're Marching to Zion," stanza 4.

# Appendix

# The Edwin T. Dahlberg Peace Award

Rev. Edwin T. Dahlberg (1892–1986) embodied a holistic commitment to personal growth and public service in Jesus Christ. Rev. Dahlberg's ministry was broad, inclusive, and compassionate, reaching into every area of life where Christian love could bring transformation. At times his passion for mission made him as controversial as the radical gospel he preached and practiced.

God's world was Dahlberg's mission field, and God's people were his congregation. A social reformer and peace activist, he was also a church pastor who welcomed people of all races during a time of segregation and civil rights controversies. As a denominational and ecumenical leader, Dahlberg's integrity as a man of faith and vision and as a laborer for peace, justice, and reconciliation remain a legacy for this and future generations.

The Edwin T. Dahlberg Peace Award is presented biannually by the American Baptist Home Mission Societies to individuals or churches for outstanding work in the cause of peace. The award is an expression of a denominational priority on biblically mandated ministries that pursue justice and freedom for all people. The work honored by the award necessarily involves positive efforts to build solid foundations for peace and the conditions that make peace possible.

First given in 1964 and presented annually in the subsequent decade, the Dahlberg Peace Award has been a symbol of the ongoing challenge for people of faith to strive for reconciliation and understanding across our conflict-ridden communities and nations. The award honors women and men who have taken up that challenge and made peacemaking a cornerstone of their witness as disciples of Jesus Christ.

## Edwin T. Dahlberg Peace Award Recipients

**1964  Martin Luther King Jr.,** for constructive work for peace with justice and freedom

**1965  L. Kijungluba Ao,** for efforts to end violence in Nagaland (India)

**1966  W. Alvin Pitcher,** for constructive work for civil rights and economic justice

**1967  Kyle Hazelden,** for leadership in opposing the Vietnam War and race relations

**1968  Leon Sullivan,** for promoting economic justice and ending apartheid in South Africa

**1969  Zelma George,** for her leadership in a successful job corps center

**1970  Frank M. Coffin,** for international development assistance

**1971  George (Shorty) Collins,** for a life championing peace with justice and freedom

**1972  Harold E. Stassen,** for his role in formulating the United Nations charter

**1973  William Sloane Coffin,** for his leadership in opposing the Vietnam War

**1975  Mabel Martin,** for work as ABCUSA representative to the United Nations

**1977  Robert Hingson,** for his medical work in eradicating epidemics

**1979  Jimmy Carter,** for his role in bringing about the Camp David accords

**1981  Gustavo Parajon,** for his peace and development work in Nicaragua

**1983  Anna Dorothy Wylie,** for her role in promoting the nuclear weapons freeze

**1985  George W. Hill,** for helping launch the National Peace Academy

**1987  George (Nick) Carter,** for advocacy of the nuclear weapons freeze

**1989  Lucius Walker,** for his work through Pastors for Peace and Interreligious Foundation for Community

**1991  Carl and Olive Tiller,** for their lifetime commitment to peacemaking

**1993  Margaret (Peg) Sherman,** for work as ABCUSA representative to the United Nations

**1995  Ken Sehested,** for his work as executive director of the Baptist Peace Fellowship of North America

**1997  Marian Wright Edleman,** for leadership of the Children's Defense Fund

**1999  Mary Ruth Crook and Roger Crook,** for their work in peace and justice ministries

**2001  Gordon Bennett and Mark Hatfield,** for their longtime peace and justice work

**2003  U.S. Congressman John Lewis of Georgia,** for longtime work for peace and justice from the civil rights movement

**2005  Hon. Charles Z. Smith,** for exceptional dedication and commitment to national and international peace and justice efforts

**2007  Dee Dee M. Coleman,** for her multicultural, ecumenical urban ministry with high-risk youth, ex-offenders, substance abusers, and others

**2009  Thomas Adams,** for his work with Chance for Life Organization, offering programs to help inmates make a successful transition back into the community

# Index